Values and
Beliefs

Values and Beliefs DUNB

A Study of
American and Norwegian
College Students

By Christen T. Jonassen

Universitetsforlaget
Oslo · Bergen · Tromsö

ISBN 82 00 04603 6

Printed in Norway
by Universitetsforlagets trykningssentral

CONTENTS

Preface 7

I   Introduction 12

II   Political Beliefs, Values and Ideology 25

III Religious Beliefs and Values of Norwegian and
     American Students 33

IV   War and Peace 40

V   American and Norwegian Students' Values and Beliefs
     Related to Higher Education 46

VI   Occupational Values 57

VII Life Satisfactions and Success 74

VIII Some Basic Value Orientations, Attitudes and Beliefs 78

IX   Summary and Conclusions 87

     Appendix A: Background Data Tables 92

     Appendix B: Questionnaire in English and Norwegian 101

PREFACE

his is a study of values and attitudes of students in two modern democrac-
acies, Norway and the United States. My interest in the comparative study
f societal values, their persistence and their change was originally stimu-
ated by research on Norwegian immigrants in the United States, which ap-
eared in 1947 as The Norwegians in Bay Ridge. At that time Marxian structur-
lism, ecological interpretation and Freudian psychology were important
neories for the understanding of social phenomena; but none of these ap-
roaches was adequate to account for the social structure, social personality
nd cultural forms that I found in the Norwegian immigrant community. The
entrality of values as social and personality determinants became salient
uring that research, and I was struck by the survival of Norwegian values
ver time, as well as in the transplantation of them to the radically different
nilieu of Brooklyn, New York.

I had, of course, been alerted to the importance of values in the analy-
is of social phenomena by the theories of Max Weber and Talcott Parsons.
ome sixteen years later value persistence, which had been so striking in
he Norwegian case, was also found to be true of Americans by Martin Lipset,
vho argued convincingly in The First New Nation (1963) that the basic value
system solidified in the early days of the United States accounts for the
hanges in and the nature of American character and institutions. He gener-
lized from these findings that once historical events have established val-
es and predispositions, these in turn become the determinants of later
vents and the direction of social change.

A contrary point of view holds that attitudes, opinions, beliefs and val-
es are chameleonic, always colored by the kaleidoscope of events or
changing structures. The question of the stability of values is relevant here,
since the data on Norwegian attitudes and values were gathered in 1962-
963, and much has happened in student worlds since. Would college stu-
ents today respond to our questions as they then did? Obviously, they

would not with regard to many of the sectors of life about which we question them. That earlier period, now almost a decade removed, was dominated i ternationally by the Cold War and the almost hot war of the Cuban missile crisis of 1962. American respondents reflected the dilemma of dual comm ment to resist Communist expansion at all costs and also to preserve peace

Student life proceeded then in its traditional ways with little or no wa ing of the worldwide student revolutions that were to occur in 1969 and 197C In the interval, the greatest change has probably occurred among American students. Studies in attitudes of American students in the earlier period showed them to be politically apathetic and conservative. In those days they pursued marks and careers as usual, and got their excitement from sex, beer, panty-raids and football. There were no signs of the sit-ins, riots, demonstrations, confrontations and political actions which occurred on hun dreds of American campuses in 1969 and 1970, and which radicalized and politicized great numbers of students who became activists in many causes. Yet the potentialities for student activism were indicated by both the Norwe gian and American data, as the quest for meaningful causes was even then evident.

When we collected data at the University of Oslo in 1962-1963 the atmo sphere was relatively placid; conservatives controlled the student govern- ment, and students and faculty went about their appointed tasks in traditiona ways. When I was there in 1970 the atmosphere was roiled with tension, demonstrations and confrontations. Wall newspapers, like those in the Chinese cultural revolution, covered the walls, exhorting students to wage the class struggle against the exploiting 'capitalists' and 'imperialists' who according to the writers, controlled the University and Norwegian society. Radicals had captured the student government and university committees were rife with dissent as students demanded, received and exercised powei they had never had before. Certainly, these students would have responded differently, if they had been willing to respond at all.

Was the student 'revolt' in both countries then a negation of the old so- cietal value system, a dramatic insistence on new values and a negation of the theory of value persistence? The student 'revolts' might with just as grea validity be interpreted as the pursuit of key values rooted in the histories o both nations. Lipset found the key American values — equality and achieve ment — to stem from that country's revolutionary origins. And America is a nation of immigrants who in the new nation sought freedom from oppressive class systems and compulsory military service. The disastrous Vietnam war compelled young Americans to fight an unpopular foreign war, compromised such key American values as achievement, freedom and morality, and seriously retarded the realization of equality. It was against the negation of key societal values, not those values themselves, that students protested. In Norway such men as Hauge, Wergeland, Bjørnson, Ibsen, Tranmael and Øverland are some links in the unbroken chain of intellectual radicals stretching from the early nineteenth century to the present. All of them castigated the establishment and championed social morality, social justice and equality for all at home and in the world. Moreover, opposition to whomever happens to be the establishment seems to be a tradition of Norwegian student society. For example, in 1962-1963, when the Labor Party was in power, the students were relatively conservative; in 1970, when a Conservative coalition governed, they were radical. Many of the older generation, dedicated socialists who have fought for and seen many of their ideals achieved in Norway, felt the sting of rejection and were perplexed and sometimes impatient with the younger generation, whom they accused of ignoring reality and accomplishments while engaging in 'romantic revolutionary' activity. Thus, while there undoubtedly have been changes in some specific students' attitudes and opinions, central and key societal values are persistent, and what appears to be a revolutionary departure may be merely a reinterpretation, a new expression of traditional values, and a protest at the discrepancy between stated values and what students perceive to be conditions at variance with these values.

In undertaking this study, I sought, by a more systematic sampling and rigorous methodology, to check certain tendencies of the Norwegian value system and differences between that system and the American one, which I had observed during my earlier investigations of Norwegian immigrants and culture in an American urban setting. This task was made possible by a Fulbright Research award which permitted me to spend a year in Norway. A grant from The Ohio State University Mershon Committee enabled me to employ assistants for interviewing, coding and statistical computations. In this work Magister Sigurd Skirbekk performed his many duties as research associate with great diligence and competence, as did research assistants Mie Ingvaldsen and Hanne Christine Thorsen.

The project profited greatly from the kind cooperation of Erik Rinde, Director of the Institute for Social Research in Oslo, who put the excellent research resources of the Institute at my disposal. I am grateful to Dagfinn Aas for his facilitation of administrative aspects and to the many members of the Institute with whom I discussed various aspects of the study. Publica tion of the monograph was financed by a grant from the Norwegian Research Council for Science and the Humanities (Norges Almenvitenskapelige Forsk- ningsråd).

Knowledge accumulates by one research building on another and this in- vestigation builds on the work of the Cornell Value Study Group. Two books, Occupations and Values by Morris Rosenberg and What College Students Thi by Rose K. Golden, Morris Rosenberg, Robin M. Williams, Jr. and Edward A. Suchman, were particularly useful.

I am indebted to my wife, Lillian, for her critical reading of the manu- script and for her help in typing it. Thanks are also due to the many anony- mous student respondents who patiently endured our many probing questions

A slightly revised version of Chapter II was published as 'A comparison of political beliefs of college students in Norway and the United States' in Acta Sociologica in 1966. In this article I point out that student responses in 1962 forecast the defeat of the Labor Party in 1965. No other part of the monograph has been published and it is essentially as it was when completed the spring of 1963.

In addition to whatever contribution this study will make to the compara tive scientific study of values, I hope it will facilitate mutual understanding between the two democracies, and contribute to greater insight in adminis- trators and faculties in both countries who are concerned with higher educati

In a preface to What College Students Think, Paul Lazarsfeld remarked that historians and classic studies of civilizations had to depend on material that had just accidentally survived, and he noted that 'When, fifty years after the French revolution, Tocqueville described the pre-revolutionary society, he (Tocqueville) stated that nothing could really be said about the peasants because there were no traces of their way of life and their political outlook.'

Something can be said about an earlier outlook of American and Norwe- gian students because systematic research was done prior to the student rev olution. Only if we have valid baselines can we begin to devise studies which will answer such questions as: which values and beliefs change over time,

hich persist regardless of events, which kind of events cause which changes
nd in what sectors of a society's value system are these alterations most
isible?

Christen T. Jonassen
The Ohio State University
1971

INTRODUCTION

Americans and Norwegians have much in common since their ways of life a derived from common cultural springs, Judaic-Christian religious tradition European enlightenment, humanism and scientific rationalism. However, their historical experience is vastly different. Norway is a small mountainous country on the edge of the Arctic Circle with few resources and a popula tion about equal to one of the boroughs of New York City, while the United States is a continental nation with many millions of people and vast resource of all kinds. American culture has been affected by waves of millions of im migrants, while Norway has been relatively free from such influence. Norway is now and was from 1935 to 1965 governed by a Labor Party with a socialist program, while the United States represents capitalism and private enterprise. Norway might be described as a welfare state committed to a wide program of state controls and social welfare, and the United States, while ideologically committed to rugged individualism and laissez-faire eco nomics, seems reluctantly to adopt more and more programs of social wel fare and state control.

Are there wide differences in the values and attitudes of young people socialized in societies so different in size, resources, ideological commit ment, economic institutions, governmental functions and historical experi ence, or do values derived from their common Western cultural heritage pe sist despite these differences to produce similarities in value orientation?

The comparative study of values in different nations should give us clu as to conflict potentials or bases for cooperation which may exist among so cieties. The origins of conflict among groups and nations are many and con plex, and may be caused by contentions for power or authority, by the strug gle for economic advantage or because of traditional animosities between persons and groups. Societal values and beliefs have often provoked and sustained vicious and prolonged conflicts in the history of wars and revolu tions, and today mankind is threatened with annihilation because of ideologi differences between communism and democracy. Conflict may have its origins in economics or political areas of life as Marx contended; however, values, beliefs and ideologies always become involved, either as the basis of the conflict or as the justification and legitimization of it and whatever abominations or sacrifices the struggle may entail.

The importance of values in determining social structure, cultural forms and personality characteristics is salient in the theoretical formulations of Max Weber and Talcott Parsons, and Seymour Lipset follows their theoretical conviction when he states that 'basic alterations of social character or values are rarely produced by changes in the means of production, distribution, and exchange alone.'[1] He sees, on the other hand, institutional arrangements making adjustments to new conditions within the framework of a dominant value system because 'changes in the dominant value system develop slowly—or not at all.'[2]

The beliefs, values and ideologies of persons and groups are the springs of action as well as the directives of it, for these ideational orientations tell them whether to act, how to act and why they should act. Behind social action are feelings about the moral rightness of the acts.

Johnson points out that in a broad sense motivation includes values, norms and cognitive assumptions (knowledge) and beliefs.[3]

Knowledge and beliefs are concerned with what exists or what people believe exists. When we ask a respondent to react to such a statement as: 'Political candidates are as a rule controlled by a political machine,' the response indicates what is thought to be true. We shall think of cognitive beliefs which can be and have been fully empirically tested as knowledge, and ideas about reality which cannot be scientifically tested and have not so been confirmed as beliefs. When we ask respondents about their concept of God, we get a statement of belief.

Values, on the other hand, are what Williams calls 'standards of desirability' by which a person or group may judge 'what is good, bad, beautiful

1. Seymour Martin Lipset, The First New Nation: The United States in Historical and Comparative Perspective, New York: Basic Books, Inc., 1963, p. 103.

2. Ibid.

3. Harry M. Johnson, Sociology: A Systematic Introduction. New York: Harcourt Brace, 1960, p. 159.

or ugly, pleasant or unpleasant, appropriate or inappropriate.'[4] When we ask a person to make a choice as to what he would rather be: independent, successful or well-liked, he is <u>evaluating</u> qualities of existence, and making a choice of what to him is the most desirable one. One can believe that something like crime exists without thinking it appropriate, and one can believe that there are societies without conflict.

<u>Values</u> and <u>beliefs</u>, though they may be distinct, are often intermingled The statement 'Social justice can be achieved only in a socialist country' involves evaluation of something called social justice and a statement about what is or is not a reality, namely that it can be obtained only in a socialist country. If one values social justice and considers the last part of the statement to be knowledge, that is, a proved cognitive assumption, then one would also presumably hold that a socialist society would be desirable or an object of value. One might be led to believe that the statement is true because one is already comitted to both social justice and socialism.

We shall also be interested in comparing the cultural <u>norms</u> of the two countries. We think of norms as being specifications or rules about what should or should not be done by persons or institutions. When we ask a person to agree or disagree with such a statement as this: 'The individual employer should sacrifice the right (to hire and fire without restriction) for the social welfare,' we are asking what the norm or rule of behavior should be for the incumbent of a social role, an employer, in a certain social situation There may be social norms that are valued by some sectors of society and not by others. The fact that the racial etiquette norms are highly valued by some Southerners but not by the colored minority group results in serious social conflict. Norms therefore are not synonymous with values, though effective social norms are usually also considered objects of value by a plurality in the society.

While we are interested in discrete values and beliefs, we shall be as interested in comparing <u>value systems</u>, because values do not usually appear in isolation but in clusters or in systems wherein the separate values have systematic relations to each other. Will students of the two countries exhibit similar or different value systems? Will certain specific beliefs and values

---

4.   For one of the best treatments of values in a sociological sense see Robin M. Williams, Jr., <u>American Society</u>, 2nd ed., New York: Alfred A. Knopf, 1960, Chap. XI, pp. 397-468.

end to be similarly related in systems, or will values and beliefs combine
in different relations in the two countries? For example, does a belief about
the essential cooperativeness and helpfulness of human nature go together
with a high evaluation of certain features of a socialist state, or do a high
valuation of freedom of individual action and a belief in laissez-faire eco-
omics belong to the same value systems in both countries, or are they re-
ated in a different fashion?

Societies have values, beliefs and knowledge with regard to all manner
of things. It is an impossible task for an investigator to analyze and compare
all the cultural norms and values of two societies, and we shall therefore
enter our inquiry on certain beliefs and values related to institutional norms,
those relatively stable obligatory prescriptions for behavior which meet the
major needs of a society and which 'constitute the essential structure by
which human behavior is channelized and given order and coherence.'[5]

The institutional sectors which will be compared are those that are considered basic in the sense that they have profound effects on other aspects
of culture and might therefore be regarded as being crucial in determining
whether there shall be consensus or conflict, tension or equanimity, between
societies. We shall examine norms, values and beliefs related to these institutional sectors: education, religion, vocation, government, war and
politics. Our assumption is that the conflict potential rises as the divergence
in values and beliefs regarding institutional norms increases, and, converse-
ly, that as complete consensus is approached, the latent or overt conflict will
be minimized.

Norway is an ancient nation and as a part of Europe has been washed by
the ideological tides of the intellectual and ideational world through the ages.
And each tide has left its residue in the consciousness and belief of some sectors of the population. Ideationally it is complex, with a diversity of interests, values, beliefs and knowledge. It is therefore hazardous to speak of the
value and belief systems of Norway, and to achieve greater confidence in our
results, we should confine our characterization to carefully delimited societal
segments which can be described with some precision.

In this study we chose what we consider to be an important and strategic
sector of the population: those who, by virtue of their societal roles, will be

5. Ibid., p. 34.

decision-makers and those who will have an impact on the attitudes and val ues of others. We felt that the students constituted a strategic group, because it is from this group that the majority of the decision- and opinion-makers of the future will be drawn, and it is members of this group perhap more than any other who will influence others in their roles as teachers an leaders in communities and institutions.

Values, beliefs and norms may be discovered from the testimony of the people who hold them or from the observation of behavior in real-life situa tions. In this research we have used the first method of discovering the val ues, beliefs and norms held by Norwegian students for the purpose of comparing them with American students. We seek to determine the quality and degree of similarities and differences in the patterns of beliefs and values of American and Norwegian students through their own testimony. But are students willing to express what they really believe, or is what they say merely rationalization or a desire to present an acceptable facade of opinio to the public view? We tried to avoid this problem by making the responses anonymous. Some would hold that American students were more willing to reveal their real thinking than Norwegian students. Evidence from our results does not seem to show that Norwegian students are more reluctant to express unconventional views. For example, more Norwegian than Americ students state that they are atheists and fewer state that they believe in the traditional God.

The question has also been raised frequently as to whether or not a sta ment of value really determined an action in accordance with the expressed belief. Arthur Schlesinger, Jr., for example, states:

> What does a public opinion poll report? It reports essentially, I would suppose, what people think they think. It does not report what people really think, because people ordinarily don't know what they really think in advance of a situation which compels them to act on the basis of their thoughts. Public opinion policy, in short, elicits essentially an irresponsible expression of opinion — irresponsible because no action is intended to follow expression. The expression of opinion is not given weight or substance by a sense of accountability for consequences; when that sense of accountability enters their expression may very likely be different. [6]

---

6. Arthur Schlesinger, Jr. The humanist looks at empirical social research, American Sociological Review, Vol. 27 (Dec. 1962), p. 769.

We can agree that people do not know exactly how they will behave in
he future, but we do believe that how they will behave is not entirely determined by the situation 'which compels them to act on the basis of their
noughts', but to some extent by what they have experienced, what they value
nd what they believe. To think otherwise would be to dismiss as immaterial
he religious, ethical, value and moral systems of societies. While situa-
ons compel, the evidence, as a historian should know, seems to be over-
helming that individuals motivated by certain values and beliefs often over-
ide the compulsion of a situation. It seems reasonable to believe that in an
nonymous situation people will state what they do believe rather than what
hey do not believe, and furthermore that what they believe will have im-
ortant consequences for their behavior even if their values do not completely
etermine their actions. 'No student of human conduct can accept uncritically,
s final evidence, people's testimony as to their own values. Yet actions may
eceive as well as words, and there seems no reason for always giving one
recedence over the other.'[7] We therefore hold that declarations of what is
rue, desirable and good are social facts which constitute important factors
n the motivations of individuals, groups and nations.

Schlesinger rightly points out the irresponsibility involved in the expres-
ion of an opinion when no action is intended to follow the expression. We
ried to avoid this problem and give weight and substance to the expressed
eliefs by placing selected questions to student respondents within what could
e to them a meaningful and vitally important frame of reference, namely
heir education, their choice of vocation and what they hope to get out of life.
tudents are certainly aware of the importance of the vocational choice they
re in the process of making; they are in a sense gambling their lives on the
hoice of a vocation, for they know it will determine how and where they will
pend the greater part of their lives and what that life will be like. If we ask
hem questions relating to war and peace they are also vitally involved, be-
ause they are the soldiers, and the wives and girl friends of the soldiers,
n any future war. Thus by asking the kind of questions that concern them
eeply, we hoped to create a sense of responsibility for the consequences
f the beliefs and values they express. By using as respondents students
vho have committed themselves, or who are in the process of so doing, we

---

. Robin M. Williams, Jr., op.cit., p. 405.

have a situation of some responsibility in which expressed belief should be related to potential behavior.

The Questionnaire

We investigated studies of values, beliefs and attitudes of Americans f the purpose of finding reliable data on the areas of culture and institutiona life which we thought were crucial. This is a vast literature, and much ex cellent research is available, but a series of studies sometimes referred t as the 'Cornell Value Studies'[8] seemed to be most suitable for our purpose They deal with the values of American students with reference to a wide range of cultural and institutional factors—the methodology used in the va ious studies is comparable, and the data given in publications are in a forn which makes statistical comparison possible. Furthermore, important cor clusions from these studies are presented and evaluated in two volumes, What College Students Think[9] and Occupation and Values. [10]

It was from these studies that we drew the majority of our questions. The schedule was first prepared in English and then translated into Norwegian. We wanted to achieve as good a basis for comparison as possible and were aware of the difficulties of translating questions so that they would mean the same to Norwegians as to Americans. We required not merely a translation that was literally correct, but one which would enable the Norw gian student to make the correct interpretation within his cultural frame of reference. It required, therefore, a translator who was not only sensitive to the sociological, psychological and theoretical phenomena that we were investigating, but also one who had mastered both languages and who had lived for some time in the societies and cultural milieus of both sets of re spondents. We were fortunate in finding a person with such qualifications to make our translation. [11] This translation was checked by sociologists fa miliar with both languages and countries. The questionnaire was then used

8. For a bibliography of these studies see Rose K. Goldsen, Morris Rose berg, Robin M. Williams, Jr. and Edward A. Suchman, What College Students Think, Princeton, N.J.: D. Van Nostrand, 1960, pp. 230, 2:

9. Goldsen et al., op. cit.

10. Morris Rosenberg, with Edward A. Suchman and Rose K. Goldsen, Occupation and Values. Glencoe, Illinois: Free Press, 1958.

11. The translator was Magister Mari Ruge of the Institute for Social Re search in Oslo.

Table 1.1. Students enrolled in Norwegian institutions
of higher learning, autumn 1961*

Institution of Higher Learning	Number	Percent
The University of Oslo	6,438	58.62
The University of Bergen	1,240	11.29
Independent Theological College	250	2.28
State Veterinary College	140	1.27
State College of Agriculture	281	2.56
State Institute of Technology	1,947	17.73
The Norwegian School of Economics and Business Administration	186	1.69
State College for Teachers	501	4.56
Totals	10,983	100.00

*   Data from: Statistisk Sentralbyrå,
              Statistisk Årbok for Norge 1962,
              Oslo, 1962, Table 346, p. 276.

in a pilot study of students, corrected for ambiguities in wording and translation and a final version prepared. Copies of the questionnaire in both languages may be found in Appendix B.

Sample: Norwegian

As indicated above, we decided to draw our sample from Norwegian students. Norwegians could then get higher education at either the University of Oslo, which had an enrollment of 5,161 students in 1961, or the University of Bergen, with an enrollment of 1,240 in the same year. In 1961, therefore there were a total of 6,632 university students in Norway. In addition, higher education in special areas is given in the technical colleges such as the Norwegian School of Economics and Business Administration in Bergen or the State Institute of Technology in Trondheim. The enrollment in Norwegian schools of higher education in 1961 is shown in Table 1.1 and gives an indication of the distribution of students.

The Norwegian students referred to here constitute a randomly selected sample drawn primarily from the University of Oslo, but since it was felt that business organization students might differ somewhat from the general run of university students in Oslo, a proportionate number of students from the Norwegian School of Economics and Business Administration in Bergen was also included in our Norwegian student sample.

In the autumn of 1962, when the research was undertaken, the University of Oslo had a total enrollment of 7,373 graduate and undergraduate students. Our aim was to match the proportion of students in samples of American universities and get a 6 percent sample. We distributed 480 questionnaires. Refusals constituted about 10 percent; in addition, incomplete schedules, withdrawals and miscellaneous causes reduced this number to 396 usable schedules. To this number were added twelve randomly selected cases from the Norwegian School of Economics and Business Administration, making a total of 408 for our Norwegian student sample. This number constitues 5.5 percent of the enrollment of the University of Oslo.

The sample was drawn from a list of students resident at Studentbyen or the student town of Oslo. This student housing is financed in part by the communes of Norway, which buy rooms or apartments to assure their students

12. The University of Oslo, Nytt fra Universitetet i Oslo, nr. 2, 1963.

Table 1.2. Comparison of curricula of students of the University
of Oslo, Norwegian School of Economics and Business Administration,
State Veterinary College and Norwegian student sample, 1962

Curricula (Faculties)	Univ. of Oslo School of Econom. and Bus. Adm., Veterinary College*		Norwegian student sample	
	No.	Percent	No.	Percent
Theology	81	1.1	6	1.3
Law	804	10.5	18	4.4
Economics	211	2.7	6	1.3
Political Science	86	1.1	7	1.7
Medicine	622	8.1	31	7.6
Philology	2,755	35.8	153	37.5
Psychology	319	4.1	13	3.2
Sociology	32	0.4	1	0.3
Physical Sciences	2,083	27.1	115	28.2
Accounting	37	0.5	0	0.0
Pharmacy	132	1.7	12	2.9
Dentistry	211	2.7	16	3.9
Veterinary Medicine	124	1.6	11	2.7
Economics and Business Adm.	200	2.6	13	3.2
No data	--	---	16	1.3
Totals	7,697	100	408	99.5

* Statistisk Sentralbyrå, Statistisk Årbok for Norge, 1962, p. 276.

of housing in a city where housing is expensive and very difficult to obtain. Since we thought it important to question representatives from all over the country because of the considerable variation between the different parts, this method of selection ensured, as can be seen from Table 1.3, that we would have representation from all parts of Norway. From the list of students every other name was drawn to be interviewed; our group therefore constitutes a 50 percent sample of students at Studentbyen. Students were asked to fill out the questionnaire and seal it in an envelope which was later collected by members of the research office.

How representative of the students of the University of Oslo is this sample? To determine this definitively, we would have to have actual counts of students on a great number of variables such as sex, home area, college courses, occupation and income of father, etc. As this report is written, few official figures are available which describe the university population, but from those which are available it would seem to be satisfactorily representative. For example, our sample had 31 percent females and 69 percent males; the percentages based on actual counts are 29 and 71 percent respectively. If the major field of study curriculum is used as an index, it can be seen from Table 1.2 that, except for law students, who appear to be somewhat underrepresented, our sample approximates the proportions based on actual counts in most instances. A description of the sample may be found in the Appendix, Tables A. 1 to A. 11.

We are therefore confident that our sample is fairly representative of the students of the University of Oslo. Whether these students are typical of all students in the country cannot be definitely established. However, it is reasonable to believe that our sample is representative because the students of the University of Oslo constitute by far the largest proportion of university students in Norway, since the humanities, professions and physical sciences are included, as are students from all areas of Norway.

Sample: American

The Norwegian students are compared with a sample of 4,585 American college students from eleven universities[13] throughout the country. These universities were chosen because the researchers believed they are an ade-

---

13. The universities are Cornell, Dartmouth, Fisk, Harvard, Michigan, North Carolina, Texas, U.C.L.A., Wayne, Wesleyan and Yale.

Table 1.3. Home county (<u>fylke</u>) of Norwegian students in sample

County	Number	Percent
Østfold	35	8.6
Akershus	18	4.4
Oslo	35	8.6
Hedmark	18	4.4
Oppland	34	8.3
Buskerud	12	2.9
Vestfold	22	5.4
Telemark	19	4.7
Aust-Agder	11	2.7
Vest-Agder	17	4.2
Rogaland	32	7.8
Hordaland	23	5.6
Bergen	8	2.0
Sogn og Fjordane	4	1.0
Møre og Romsdal	18	4.4
Sør-Trøndelag	19	4.7
Nord-Trøndelag	8	2.0
Nordland	21	5.1
Troms	12	2.9
Finnmark	1	0.2
Abroad	2	0.5
No information	39	9.6
Totals	408	100

quate selection of the most representative types of universities in the United States, which would give the range of college student opinion in important universities and provide a standard against which other campuses might be measured.[14]

The American investigators tried to approximate national student opinion by the analysis of questionnaires from 2,975 students chosen from the total number interviewed in such a way that each university involved contributed only its proportional share to constitute a 6 percent sample of all eleven student bodies. It is this particular sample that is most often used in the American-Norwegian comparisons. In a few tables of comparison we use the full 4,585 sample. In the universities of the American sample only men were chosen except for Cornell; consequently comparisons involving different reactions of men and women are based only on Cornell women students. We attempted to control for the sex of the respondents when dealing with matters in which this was expected to create marked differences of opinion, and in which data were available for the American sample.

---

14. Goldsen et al., op. cit., p. xxvi.

II

POLITICAL BELIEFS, VALUES AND IDEOLOGY

The sharpest political divisions in this era seem to be between those who believe that individual and national welfare are best served by private initiative, rugged individualism, capitalism and a small government role in social and economic affairs, and those who hold that government should intervene to plan, control and manage the social and economic life of society for the welfare of all its citizens. Generally, the former tend to take up orthodox and traditional positions when confronted with decisions in life and are usually labelled conservatives or right-wing in politics. The latter usually go under such labels as liberals, left-wing, radicals, socialists or communists, depending on the degree of government ownership, control and activity they support.

Are Norwegian students, brought up in a 'socialist-welfare' state, more liberal than their American counterparts socialized in a 'capitalistic' society? Which students are more politically involved, sensitive, concerned and interested in public affairs? How do they stand on specific issues related to government, economics and education?

One of the most striking characteristics of the American students studied was their political apathy; they simply could not get very excited about things political.[1] As can be seen from Table 2.1, it is clear that Norwegian students are more committed and involved in politics and public affairs than are students from the American universities studied. The differences are statistically significant.

These differences probably arise because Norwegian students play a different role in society from that of American students. Each political party in Norway has its representative in student groups and the student organization sends representatives to party caucuses and nominating meetings. Norwegian students are thus, by tradition and formal organization, part of and

---

1.   Goldsen et al., op. cit., p. 218. See also Ch. 5.

Table 2.1. Proportion of positive responses of American and
Norwegian students to the question:

'Do you ever get as worked up about something that happens in
politics or public affairs as you do about something that happens in your personal life?' (Norwegian students and eleven
US universities*)

University	Percentage who said 'yes'	Total
Oslo	58	408
Wayne	46	519
Yale	44	297
Wesleyan	44	277
Cornell Men: 1952	42	655
Harvard	41	453
Dartmouth	39	365
Texas	39	516
UCLA	38	467
Michigan	38	488
Fisk	37	134
North Carolina	34	414

---

* Data for American universities from Goldsen et al., op.cit.,
p. 218.

nvolved significantly in Norway's political life. We should therefore expect hat their opinions will reflect political trends in society to a greater extent han American students.

Another central finding of the American study was that American students were conservative in their political orientations. [2] We found that Norwegian students are evenly balanced in their political preferences between right- (37.3 percent) and left- (36.3 percent) wing parties. In Table 2.2 the parties are ordered from the Conservative Party, Høyre, at the top to the most radical, the Communist, at the bottom. The Kristelig Folkeparti (the Christian People's Party) is a conservative party which has as its special aim the realization of Christian values in national life. Senterpartiet (the Agrarians) is the old farmers' party. Venstre is the Liberal Party and Det Norske Arbeiderpartiet is the Labor Party, which in 1962 had governed Norway for a generation since 1935. As a responsible government which had to administer a state and come to terms with the realities of economic and political life, the Labor Party modified its original dogmatic socialist line of government control and ownership of resources and means of production to one of government planning and control and the development of state welfare. Thus, after twenty-eight years in power, only 14 percent of economic enterprises were government-owned. This trend alienated the socialist ideologues of the party, who split away from it and formed the Sosialistisk Folkeparti (the Socialist People's Party).

We sought to determine political trends by comparing political orientations of fathers and sons. These comparisons are found in Table 2.2. The most striking difference between them is the 'loss' suffered by the Labor Party, which declines from 23.3 adherents among the fathers to 9.6 among the sons. It is clear that the biggest gainer from this loss is the Socialist People's Party, which rises from 2.5 to 6.7 percent. Where did the rest of Labor's loss go? It is probable that it is contained in the large percentage, 15.6, who are undecided and feel that no party really represents their own beliefs, or those who don't know, 10.9 percent. The large percentage (26.5) seems to reflect changing weather in the political atmosphere of Norway. And the Labor Party, which has been a strong minority party (74 out of 150) since 1961, may be in for stormy weather in the next election if students' political attachments are any indication.

2. Ibid., p. 101.

Table 2.2. Comparison of political preferences of fathers and sons

Political parties	Political preference of sons (Percentage of those responding) n = 405	Political preference of fathers (Percentage of those responding) n = 400	C.R
Høyre (H)	31.4	26.2	1.6
Kristelig Folkeparti (Kr.F)	2.9	6.0	2.1
Senterpartiet (SP)	2.9	9.8	4.0
Venstre (V)	18.8	17.0	-
Det Norske Arbeiderpartiet (DNA)	9.9	23.2	4.9
Sosialistisk Folkeparti (SF)	6.7	2.5	2.7
Norges Kommunistiske Parti (NKP)	0.9	0.8	-
None of these	15.6	2.3	6.9
Don't know	10.9	12.2	-

The Conservative Party has also gained, apparently at the expense of the Christian People's Party and the Agrarians, but this trend is not statistically significant. It should also be pointed out that the Conservative Party is the single party with the largest proportion among students. In general a polarization process seems to be in operation with parties of the extreme right and left gaining while parties of center positions like the Liberals remain the same or lose like Labor and the Agrarians.

The conservative cast of present college students in both countries is supported by the fact that the Norwegian Conservative Party has the largest representation among Norwegian students, and that American students are conservative in their outlook and beliefs. However the label 'conservative' has meaning only within the ideational and political framework of the two countries and does not tell us whether American students are really more conservative than Norwegian ones; to determine their comparative position in the political spectrum we must measure their beliefs against a standard scale of specific issues. Both sets of students were asked to answer a series of questions which have proved to be good indicators of political orientation

Table 2.3. Distribution of opinion of US and Norwegian students
on items related to economics, government, welfare and education*

Item Number and Description	Percentage expressing conservative opinions		
	US (n = 2,975)	Norway (n = 408)	C.R.
47. College education should be free to everyone who can profit from it. Disagree	54	15	14.7
48. The best government is the one which governs least. Agree	31	13	7.5
49. Labor unions in this country are doing a fine job. Disagree	48	26	8.3
50. Government planning almost inevitably results in the loss of individual liberties and freedom. Agree	38	22	6.3
52. If people are certain of a minimum wage they might lose their initiative. Agree	35	42	2.8
53. The individual employer should sacrifice his right (to hire and fire without restriction) for the social welfare.** Disagree	61	39	8.3
54. The welfare state tends to destroy individual initiative. Agree	59	57	--
56. Democracy depends fundamentally on the existence of free business enterprise. Agree	62	39	8.8
58. The laws governing labor unions are not strict enough. Agree	40	14	10.2
60. If there is no ceiling on business profits there is a better chance to develop products at lower cost.** Agree	38	15	9.2

* Data for American students from Goldsen et al., op. cit., pp. 108, 109.
** Asked only at Cornell, 1950 (n = 2,758).

and which give indications of attitudes relative to important social and politi cal problems. These questions, together with a summary of the answers of American and Norwegian students, are found in Table 2.3.

The effect of years of socialization in a country whose government has been administered by a party oriented toward socialism, state planning an social welfare is evident in Norway as is the result of being brought up in th United States, a country where ideologies of private enterprise, individual initiative, laissez-faire economics, and local government are liberally preached if not practiced. It will be seen that with regard to every question except two a much larger proportion of Norwegian than American students take a liberal stance or a position to the left.

An interesting reversal takes place with regard to the response to the statement: 'If people are certain of a minimum wage, they might lose their initiative.' Forty-two percent of Norwegians as against 35 percent of Amer cans agreed with this statement. If we compare Oslo University students with those from the eleven US universities (Table 2.4), we see that with regard to this question the Norwegians are more conservative than students from most American universities in the sample, even more to the right than the Ivy League schools. The only American students who seem to be more conservative than the Norwegians are those from the Universities of Texas and North Carolina. Why should students of a welfare state, governed for a generation by a Labor Party, agree to a greater extent than students in a capitalist state to such a statement? Have they been negatively affected by observing the results of a minimum wage policy? It is interesting also that the majority of students of both countries agree to the same degree that 'the welfare state tends to destroy individual initiative.' Does this mean that the next generation of Norwegian political leaders will tend to alter wage and in centive policies toward a position more in accordance with conservative policy?

There are great variations in response to the statements in Table 2.4 among the eleven US universities. The American students who most nearly approach the liberal tendencies of the Norwegians are from Fisk (black), Wayne (city) and the liberal Ivy League colleges; the most conservative came from North Carolina and Texas. Harvard and Oslo Universities are both liberal, but they definitely part company on two statements: 'Democrac

related to economic philosophy, economic issues and government responsibility for education and welfare*

(Percentages expressing conservative opinions)

Item Number and Description	Univ. of Oslo (408)	Tested US Univs. (2,975)	Cor-nell Men (655)	Dart-mouth (365)	Fisk (134)	Har-vard (453)	Michi-gan (488)	North Caro-lina (414)	Texas (516)	UCLA (467)	Wayne (519)	Wes-leyan (277)	Yale (297)
47. College education should be free to everybody. Disagree	15	54	59	68	44	57	62	63	49	33	46	66	65
48. The best government is the one which governs least. Agree	13	31	32	26	27	29	30	33	35	29	29	32	32
49. Labor unions in this country are doing a fine job. Disagree	26	48	37	48	19	35	45	49	43	32	33	40	43
50. Government planning almost inevitably results in the loss of individual liberties and freedom. Agree	22	38	34	30	20	23	32	34	40	30	25	25	38
52. If people are certain of a minimum wage, they might lose their initiative. Agree	42	35	32	38	34	23	36	51	45	27	31	34	36
53. The individual employer should sacrifice his right (to hire and fire without restriction) for the social welfare.** Disagree	39	-	61	-	-	-	-	-	-	-	-	-	-
54. The welfare state tends to destroy individual initiative. Agree	57	59	60	63	32	48	69	63	60	55	56	57	64
56. Democracy depends fundamentally on the existence of free business enterprise. Agree	39	62	62	59	53	46	67	72	70	61	62	62	60
58. The laws governing labor unions are not strict enough. Agree	14	40	52	55	22	43	54	51	45	42	40	61	55
60. If there is no ceiling on business profits there is a better chance to develop products at lower costs.** Agree	15	-	38	-	-	-	-	-	-	-	-	-	-

* Data for the American students from Goldsen et al., op. cit., p. 108.

** Asked only at Cornell, 1950.

depends fundamentally on the existence of free business enterprise' and 'Th laws governing labor unions are not strong enough.' With regard to these statements a much larger proportion of Harvard students than Oslo student take the conservative position and agree with each statement.

Summary

The political involvement of the Norwegian students and the apathy of th American students probably results from the fact that the United States giv its students no meaningful role in the political life of the nation, [3] while Nor does so. Within the political and ideological framework of their separate countries, students from both nations have conservative tendencies, but judged against the scale of specific issues, Norwegian students are much more to the left except on the issue of a guaranteed minimum wage and the effects on initiative of the welfare state. The effects of the ideological orie tation of the two countries are thus in the main reflected in the attitudes of their students. Among Norwegian students there seems to be a decided swi away from the Labor Party and a slight trend away from the parties of the center to those of the extreme right and left, but many are undecided, indi- cating a shifting political climate.

---

3. The lowering of the voting age to eighteen in the US in 1971 changed thi situation.

III

RELIGIOUS BELIEFS AND VALUES OF NORWEGIAN AND AMERICAN STUDENTS

The nature of religious institutions, organization and education differs greatly in the two countries. Norway has a state religion, Lutheranism, while the United States has, quantitatively speaking, three major faiths, Protestant, Catholic and Jewish, and many minor ones, and within the Protestant faith there are a number of large independent denominations.

Many Americans receive no systematic religious instruction, some get one hour or so a week in Sunday School and a minority are exposed to continuous systematic religious instruction in parochial schools, mainly Catholic. On the other hand, when a Norwegian student arrives at the university, at about the age of nineteen or twenty, he has had continuous systematic religious instruction since he started elementary school at seven years of age and all through secondary school. One should expect that this training would have an important effect and that therefore Norwegian students would be more religious than American ones. We found the opposite to be true: Norwegian students are much less religious than American students.

Dimensions of Religiousness

How did we arrive at this conclusion and what is 'religiousness?' We defined religiousness within the conceptual framework developed by the Cornell Value Study Project.[1] This approach was particularly suitable because we wanted to obtain a valid basis of comparison between American and Norwegian students, and because this theoretical approach has been validated by considerable empirical research.[2] This conceptual framework specifies four facets of 'religiousness':

1. Cf. Goldsen et al., op. cit., Ch. 7, pp. 153-168.
2. Loc. cit., pp. 169-195.

1. Belief in a superhuman, supernatural Deity, a 'Divine God.'
2. Identification with and personification of the person's religious group.
3. Commitment to religious activity as a major source of satisfaction in life.
4. Feeling of a need for religious faith.

When used in a Guttman-type scale, the pattern of responses to those questions eliciting information on these factors fitted the criteria for a scale,[3] that is, they referred to the same trait defined as 'religiousness.' It should be noted that this scale appears to have the advantage of being free from a reference to any set of ideas or doctrines uniquely associated with any of the three major faiths, and all factors might be considered compatibl with Protestant, Catholic or Jewish teachings.[4] Within this conceptual fram work, then, the dimensions of religiousness were measured in terms of the students' response to questions eliciting information relative to the factor.

Concept of Deity and Secularization

If one is to judge by the universal occurrence of 'religious' activity, ma seems to be the kind of creature who has the need to believe in some orderin power or idea greater than and outside of himself. Religious belief systems seem to have as an essential aspect recognition of a superhuman power. In most religions this power is seen as an anthropomorphic omnipotent God. A beliefs about godliness depart from this position to belief in some other idea or controlling agent such as 'nature', 'science' or 'humanity' as the source of power and goodness, there is a retreat from a religious orientation to a secular one based on social morality and ethics. We sought to test the rela tive position of students by a series of questions[5] graded from orthodox be lief in the Deity at one end of the scale to atheism at the other. These ques tions and the responses of American and Norwegian students to them are shown in Table 3.1.

---

3. Loc.cit., p. 159.
4. Loc.cit., p. 160.
5. Similar questions have been used in a number of studies in the United States. See Goldsen et al., op.cit.; also D. Katz and K. Allport, Student Attitudes (Syracuse, N.Y.: The Craftsman Press, 1931, p. 259) and Murray Ross, The Religious Beliefs of Youth (New York: Associated Press, 1950).

Table 3.1. Ideas of the Deity among American and Norwegian students
(Percentages choosing indicated statements)

Statement	American* (N = 2,975)	Norwegian (N = 408)	C.R.
1. I believe in a divine God, creator of the universe, who knows my innermost thoughts and feelings, and to whom one day I shall be accountable.	48	33	5.7
2. I believe in a power greater than myself, which some people call God and some people call nature.	27	29	0.9
3. I believe in the worth of humanity but not in God or a Supreme Being.	5	11	5.0
4. I believe in natural law, and that the so-called universal mysteries are ultimately knowable according to scientific method.	7	8	-
5. I am not quite sure what I believe. (Agnostic)	12	14	1.2
6. I am an atheist.	1	5	6.3
	100	100	

---

*   Data for American students from Goldsen et al., op. cit., p. 154.

It will be seen that less than 50 percent of students believe in a 'divine' God, Creator of the universe, who knows my innermost thoughts and feelin and to whom one day I shall be accountable.' A significantly larger propor- tion (48 percent as against 33 percent) of American students believe in such a God. Americans, then, to a greater extent than Norwegian students, take what might be described as a religious view of godliness.

A more secular view is expressed by statements 2, 3 and 4. The per- centage of American students who adhere to these views is 39 and of Norwe gians 48. The Norwegian students' view of the Deity as compared to the Americans' might be described as predominantly secular rather than religi

The two samples of students do not differ significantly regarding the pr portion of agnostics (12 and 14 percent). The proportions of professed athe ists are small in both samples, but about five times as many Norwegians a Americans said they were atheists.

Commitment to and Evaluation of Religious Activity

We tried to determine the relative position of religion in the hierarchy of values of American and Norwegian students by asking the question: 'Wha three things or activities in your life do you expect to give you the most sat isfaction?' We also asked them to rank these activities in the order of thei importance.[6] Both Norwegian and American students give religion a fairly low rating together with leisure time and recreational activities, only abou 5 percent giving it a rating of first importance. They are very much alike also in their placement of religion in the 'low' category, with 83 percent of American and 85 percent of Norwegians indicating their expectation that re ligion will be a source of low satisfaction for them. The slight difference b tween Americans and Norwegians is not statistically significant, and we ca therefore be confident that they are similar in their negative evaluation of religion as a source of major life satisfaction.

American investigators found religious beliefs on campuses of the Unit States widespread, but characterized the philosophical climate of the cam- puses as essentially non-religious, and religious values as 'broadly dispers highly personal, relative and vague' and found that these values were only

---

6. See Table 7. 1.

weakly engaged in other spheres of life.[7] They state '... there is an even
more marked absence of intense commitment to it (religon)'[8]

Table 3.2. Religiousness of American* and Norwegian students
(Percentages expressing agreement)

Item number	American (n = 2,975)	Norwegian (n = 408)	C.R.
69. Need for religious faith.	80	63	7.8
102 (1). 'I believe in a Divine God ...'	48	33	5.7
102 (6). I am an atheist.	1	5	6.3
70. Church or religion 'has its own personality ...'	38	28	3.9
8. Religion expected to be a major source of satisfaction in life.	17	13	2.0

*   Data for American students from Goldsen et al., op.cit., p. 159.

Identification with a Religious Group

Besides belief in a supernatural Deity and commitment to it as a life
activity, religion has its associational aspects. A group sharing the same
religious symbols and beliefs and which participates in common rituals be-
comes part of the psyche of the individuals who compose it. Thus, for the
truly religious, there is a consciousness of a religious kind, a feeling of
mystical unity with the group, which may become a characteristic personification in their minds. It will be seen from Table 3.2 that about 38 percent
of Americans and about 28 percent of Norwegians indicate that their religious
group has this type of meaning for them. Again Norwegian students in this
sense appear to be less religious than American ones.

7.   Goldsen et al., op.cit., p. 202.
8.   Loc.cit., p. 156. Emphasis mine.

Need for Religious Faith and Philosophy

A large majority of students from both nations replied in the affirma-
tive to the question: 'I feel I need to believe in some sort of religious faith
or philosophy;' Norwegians, however, did so to a significantly lesser degre
than the Americans. It might seem that this finding clashes with the negativ
or passive attitude to religion expressed by the majority of the students que
tioned, but it is probable, as Table 3.1 indicates, that students here are ex
pressing a need for faith in something and not necessarily a religious faith
in the strict sense of the word.

Summary

Although Norwegian students have much more formal, systematic train
ing in religion than American students they are less religious. While a larg
proportion accept the orthodox view of the Deity, less than 50 percent of the
students sampled in either nation believe in the type of God the major religions profess. Americans are more religious in their concept of the Deity
and Norwegians more secular; both groups are equally agnostic, but there
are more atheists among Norwegian than among American students.

There is a definite lack of intensive commitment to religion on the part
of both sets of students as compared with their commitment to family life
and career. Religious activity is ranked low in the value hierarchy of Amer
ican and Norwegian students. Americans to a greater extent than Norwegian
identified themselves with their religious group as a community of believers
In their replies to every question, Norwegians evidenced less religiousness
than did American students, but even the religiousness of American students
as indicated above, is not very religious in the real sense of commitment.

A large majority of both national groups said they felt a need to believe
in some sort of religious faith or philosophy, but this expression of need ma
merely reflect the need for something to believe in strongly and with commit
ment.

It would seem that if we take the response to this question together with
the rather negative reaction to other indications of religiousness, the major
ity of students are saying in essence, 'We feel a great need for a faith and a
philosophy, but the orthodox, traditional concept of God is not acceptable. I

do not expect to find my major life satisfactions in religion, and I therefore withhold my commitment to it. '

If the attitudes towards religion expressed by American and Norwegian students reflect the view of the youth of the Western World, those who would rally future soldiers by religious appeals had better look elsewhere for exhortations by which to motivate youth to accept the risk of annihilation for themselves and their families.

IV

WAR AND PEACE

Students of today live in the turbulence of the cold war where alternating col
and hot blasts from Moscow and Washington agitate the atmosphere. To the
war and peace is not an academic question because they have been confronte
with the possibility of serving as soldiers in a conventional war and/or of
being incinerated in an atomic war. What are their attitudes to war and pea
in this situation?

What students think of war and peace will be described in terms of thei
answers to such questions as: Under what conditions would they accept the
necessity of war? What do they think about the morality of war and how effective certain war-preventive measures might be? Are American students
more warlike or pacifist than Norwegian ones? On what points do they
agree, and on which do they differ?

The present world situation presents students, like all others, with mo
and ethical dilemmas. Is war ever justified or good? If the answer is 'no,'
how does one preserve a precious way of life against an implacable enemy
who believes in the justification of any means to the achievement of his ends
Are students idealists in believing in peace at any price, in mutual efforts
and negotiations in the UN rather than in the finite violence of the atomic
bomb? Do they think a nation's right should be founded on justice and morals
rather than might, or have they become cynical realists in response to the
violent events of our times? Are they resigned to war or do they see hope f
the efforts of men to preserve the peace?

Three quarters of the American students disagreed that there could be
'lots of good things about war' and about three fifths thought war was morali
wrong, yet three quarters also disagreed with the statement:[1] 'Human lives
are too important to be sacrificed for the preservation of any form of gover
ment.' The majority of Norwegians, 54 percent, on the other hand, agreed
with this statement (see Table 4.1).

1.   Goldsen et al., op.cit., p. 142.

Table 4.1. American and Norwegian students' responses

to statement 61:

'Human lives are too important to be sacrificed for the preservation of any form og government' (Data given as percentages)

Answers	Americans* (n = 2,975)	Norwegians (n = 408)	C.R.
Agree	12	54	21.09
Disagree	75	29	18.87
Uncertain	12	16	-
No data	1	1	-

Data for American students from Goldsen et al., op.cit., p. 142.

Table 4.2. American and Norwegian students' responses

to question 101:

'Do you think it would be worth fighting an all-out war to stop
Communism, or do you think an all-out war to stop
Communism would not be worthwhile?'
(Data given as percentages)

Answers	Americans* (n = 2,975)	Norwegians (n = 408)	C.R.
Very worthwhile	26	6	8.90
Fairly worthwhile	14	6	4.49
Undecided	12	-	-
No opinion	4	10	-
Hardly worthwhile	18	23	-
Not at all worthwhile	24	54	12.67
No answer	2	1	-

*   Data for American students from Goldsen et   al., op.cit., p. 143.

Why should there be this significant difference between the two groups of students and why the apparent reversal of principle on the part of Americans? Perhaps the answer is given by the data in Table 4.2. It is clear that a significantly greater proportion (26 as against 6 percent) of American students think it worthwhile to fight an all-out war to stop Communism while a significantly greater proportion of Norwegian students (54 as against 24 percent) think it not at all worthwhile. Thus Norwegian students might be said to be consistent in their humanistic principles, while Americans would appear to be willing to sacrifice pacificism to stop Communism. Which set of students is more idealistic depends on one's concept of the paramount values

A majority of both groups of students <u>disagreed</u> with the statement: 'Peace and war are both essential to progress, 'but a significantly larger proportion of Norwegians disagreed with it, as can be seen from Table 4.3. Table 4.5 shows that Norwegian and American students are substantially in agreement with regard to beliefs about the most effective deterrent to war. Both nations' students reject the proposition that might makes right, and both to an equal degree reject the pessimistic suggestion that 'in spite of all our efforts for peace, nations just cannot live together peacefully so we might as well expect a war every few years.'

We asked Norwegian students whether they thought rocket experiments should be conducted in secret or openly. The students were decidedly for open, non-secret experiments (72 to 10 percent) (see Table 4.4.).

A respondent's reaction to the type of questions used in this section depends, of course, on the world situation and the state of international tension at the moment of investigation. American students were questioned in 1952 during the Korean War when 76 percent of the men who were interviewed fully expected to be called up for military service shortly. [2] They were very conscious, therefore, of the personal implications of their answers and sensitive to the violence of Communist expansion tactics. Is the apparently more warlike attitude of Americans due to the fact that America was militarily engaged with its Communist enemy at that time?

Many Norwegian students responded intensely in October, November and December 1962 during the Cuban crisis when international tension was, if anything, more severe. Norwegian students felt themselves very much in-

2. Goldsen et al., op.cit., p. 140.

Table 4.3. American and Norwegian students' responses

to statement 65:

'Peace and war are both essential to progress'
(Data given as percentages)

Answers	Americans* (n = 2,975)	Norwegians (n = 408)	C.R.
Agree	25	14	4.89
Disagree	63	76	5.14
Uncertain	11	10	-
No answer	1	-	-

*   Data for American students from Goldsen et al., op. cit., p. 142.

Table 4.4. Norwegian students' responses to question 99:

'What do you think is the best way for a nation to conduct rocket
and space experiments?' (Data given as percentages)

Answers	(n = 408)
Conduct experiments as much as possible in secret and tell about them only when and if they are successful.	10
Conduct all experiments in the open with full publicity thus exposing both failures and successes.	72
One way is as good as another.	16
No data	2

involved; so much so in fact that they demonstrated in front of the American Embassy in Oslo and invaded it, disrupting a poetry reading with speeches condemning unjustified American intervention in Cuba. (This was a few days before Kruschev admitted the presence of Russian atomic rockets in Cuba.) We do not think Americans would have reacted more mildly in 1962 under the threat of Russian rockets ninety miles away in Cuba than to the danger of Communist armies across the wide Pacific. Thus, as far as international tension is concerned, the situations during which the questions were asked seem to be quite similar. In both, the personal involvement of students with the issues of the questions is obvious.

Table 4.5. Norwegian and American students' opinions on
war and related issues (Data given in percentages)

Item number and description	Answers	Americans* (n = 2,975)	Norwegians (n = 408)
59. In spite of all our efforts for peace, nations just cannot live together peacefully so we might as well expect a war every few years.	Agree	16	15
	Disagree	73	74
	Uncertain	10	11
	No data	1	1
62. A nation's rights are determined by the nation's power.	Agree	29	28
	Disagree	59	61
	Uncertain	12	10
	No data	-	-
100. Which do you, personally, count on as the most effective deterrent against war: the atom bomb or the UN?	The atom bomb	51	53
	The UN	45	44
	No answer	4	3

---

* Data for American students from Goldsen et al., op.cit., p. 143.

Summary

American students are not jingoists, nor are they like the disillusioned pacifists of the thirties who thought World War I had been caused by munition makers. Perhaps they might be described as ambivalent idealists caught between their abhorrence of war and the possible necessity to engage in it, for they hold war to be immoral and military life to be distasteful, and yet accept the necessity of hostilities to defend their way of life against Communis at the sacrifice of humanistic principles.

Norwegian students, on the other hand, are consistently strongly pacifis and would probably be most reluctant crusaders in a holy war against Communism. Both groups of students seem strong in their belief in what might be called a humanistic, idealistic and essentially pacifist ideology. The mor consistent and determined pacifism of Norwegians may be due to the strong anti-war and anti-bomb movement in the University of Oslo in 1962-1963, which was reminiscent of the peace movement and demonstrations on American campuses during the decade of 1930-1940.

V

AMERICAN AND NORWEGIAN STUDENTS'
VALUES AND BELIEFS RELATED TO HIGHER EDUCATION

That students in their concept of what the aims and function of education
should be reflect to a certain extent not only the general orientation to life
characteristic of their societies, but also values compatible with the norms
of their own subgroups, has been shown by empirical studies of American
students.[1] When we ask what the most important goals of a university should
be, we are dealing with an actual situation wherein expressed opinion is
linked in a responsible way to action by the students' own involvement in the
educational process.

We asked students to consider which of the following educational goals
an ideal college or university ought to emphasize:

a. Provide vocational training; develop skills and techniques directly applicable to your career.
b. Develop your ability to get along with different kinds of people.
c. Provide a basic general education and appreciation of ideas.
d. Develop your knowledge and interest in community and world problems.
e. Help develop your moral capacities, ethical standards and values.
f. Prepare you for a happy marriage and family life.

The students were then asked to tell us whether they thought these goals
were of high or medium importance, or if they were of low importance, irrelevant or even distasteful. In addition they were asked to rank all those
goals which they had indicated as being of high importance in the order of
their importance.[2]

We were particularly interested in testing the validity of the widely-held
stereotype of Americans and American education, namely that Americans

---

1. Cf. Goldsen et al., op. cit.
2. See Appendix B for actual wording of questions and directions.

Table 5.1. Choice of educational goals.

Percentage of American and Norwegian students ranking
college educational goals as of highest or of low importance*

Educational goal	Highest importance			Low importance		
	American (n = 2,975)	Norwegian (n = 408)	C.R.	American (n = 2, 975)	Norwegian (n = 408)	C.R.
Provide vocational training, develop skills and techniques directly applicable to your career	36	62	10.06	9	2	4.83
Develop your ability to get along with different kinds of people	17	2	7.98	3	37	24.63
Provide a basic general education and appreciation of ideas	35	22	5.47	3	5	2.14
Develop your knowledge and interest in community and world problems	3	4	1.05	6	9	2.33
Help develop your moral capacities, ethical standards and values	8	8	-	15	28	6.60
Prepare you for a happy marriage and family life	1	1	-	36	83	18.01

— Indicates less than 1 percent or C.R.'s not calculated.

* Data from Table 5.2.

are essentially pragmatic, practical and instrumentally oriented and particularly so when compared with Europeans regarding their ideas of university
education. This image of American higher education is held not only by
Europeans but by many Americans as well. Williams, for example, states
'College education is valued chiefly as a means to occupational success ...
Correspondingly relatively low (but increasing) value is attached to training
in the arts, citizenship, character development or other indoctrinating, liberal, general or humanistic studies.'[3] These are confirmed a decade later
when he holds that in America 'Education ... is serious business, and the
prime questions are: "What use is it?" "What can you do with it?"'[4] and
that 'Neither a frontier society nor a business civilization values contempla
tion and detached intellectual activity above utilitarian activity.'[5]

Whether this hypothesis holds good for the general population on closer
scrutiny we do not know, but empirical research on a cross-section of Ame
ican students shows that the goal emphasized by 74 percent of the students i
to 'provide general education and appreciation of ideas' while 60 percent thi
vocational training should be stressed.[6] American students thus negate the
generally accepted stereotype with regard to the ranking of certain educatio
goals.

There is still the question, however, of whether Americans are more i
strumental and pragmatic in their approach to education than Europeans.
Comparison with Norwegians provided part of the answer and the data definitely invalidate the stereotype. In Table 5.1 we present data on which educational goals were ranked as the single most important aim for an ideal un
versity and which ones students considered to be of little importance. It wil
be seen that 62 percent of Norwegians as against 36 percent of American st
dents ranked the utilitarian goal as the highest; and that 35 percent of Ame
icans as against 22 percent of Norwegians ranked the academic general edu
cation goal highest. Table 5.2 shows the proportions ranking certain goals
high, medium and low. Again the tendency noted above is confirmed, with
60 percent of Americans as against 85 percent of Norwegians choosing the
pragmatic goal while 74 percent of Americans as against 60 percent of

3. Robin M. Williams, Jr., American Society 1st ed., 1951, p. 296.

4. Robin M. Williams, Jr., American Society 2nd ed., 1960, p. 310.

5. Loc.cit., p. 321.

6. Goldsen et al., op.cit., pp. 5-7.

Table 5.2. Ranking of various educational goals by
American and Norwegian students (percentages)

Educational goal	American* (n = 2,975)				Norwegian (n = 408)			
	Highly important				Highly important			
	First	Other high	Medium	Low	First	Other high	Medium	Low
Provide vocational training, develop skills and techniques directly applicable to your career	36	24	31	9	62	23	13	2
Develop your ability to get along with different kinds of people	17	55	26	3	2	17	43	37
Provide a basic general education and appreciation of ideas	35	39	24	3	22	38	34	5
Develop your knowledge and interest in community and world problems	3	47	44	6	4	38	49	9
Help develop your moral capacities, ethical standards and values	8	37	40	15	8	27	36	28
Prepare you for a happy marriage and family life	1	21	42	36	1	2	13	83

_____

*   Data for the American students is taken from Goldsen et al., op. cit.,
Table 1-1, p. 7.

Norwegians emphasized the academic and appreciation-of-ideas values. Ex amination of the two Tables mentioned will show that these tendencies are confirmed by those educational goals which the students deemed to be of low value or irrelevant for a university.

It should be noted that students from both countries consider that both vocational training and general education should be emphasized in college education. Table 5.4 compares students from various universities in the United States with students from the University of Oslo. It will be seen that the percentage of Oslo University students who emphasize academic values is lower (60 percent) than for any American university involved except Fisk and that their emphasis on utilitarian vocational values is higher (85 percen than for any American university. The greatest differences can be found be tween the University of Oslo and the older eastern universities with their lo tradition of liberal education. Norwegian students in this regard are more like midwestern and western state universities.

For Americans the development of the ability to get along with differen kinds of people also appears to be a desirable goal, with 72 percent of the students ranking it as being of high importance; the corresponding propor- tion for Norwegians is only 19 percent. Thus the generally held idea that Americans are more 'other-directed' and concerned with getting along with others, and that Norwegians are less so, is confirmed by these data. This tendency is confirmed when 17 percent of Americans and only 2 percent of Norwegians deem interpersonal goals to be of the highest importance and al when 37 percent of Norwegians and only 3 percent of Americans put this goa in the 'low' category. All differences mentioned are statistically significan

Norwegians and Americans are much alike in their judgment of the role of the university in developing knowledge and interest in community and wor problems and in the relative importance of the function of developing ethical and moral standards. When it comes to developing a happy marriage and family life, more Americans than Norwegians see the latter function as bei valid for the university, and Norwegians seem definitely to reject this func- tion as a university goal since 83 percent of Norwegian as against 36 percen of American students do not consider this a valid university function. Stu- dents from both countries seem to place these functions (d, e, f) in a residua category and Norwegians also place interpersonal goals in a type of educa-

Table 5.3. Ranking of college educational goals by Norwegian students

Percentage of students ranking each goal as:

Educational goals Items 11 - 22	Highly important First		Other high		Medium (M)		Low (L)		No data		Totals	
	No.	Percent	No.	Percent	No.	Percent	No.	Percent	No.	Percent	No.	Percent
a. Provide vocational training and develop skills and techniques directly applicable to your career	254	62	93	23	53	13	7	2	1	0	408	100
b. Develop your ability to get along with different kinds of people	10	2	70	17	175	43	151	37	2	1	408	100
c. Provide a basic general education and appreciation of ideas	90	22	155	38	140	34	21	5	2	1	408	100
d. Develop your knowledge and interest in community and world problems	17	4	157	38	198	49	35	9	1	0	408	100
e. Help develop your moral capacities, ethical standards and values	34	8	109	27	148	36	115	28	2	1	408	100
f. Prepare you for a happy marriage and family life	2	1	9	2	54	13	339	83	4	1	408	100

tional function which should not be greatly emphasized by a university, whil
Americans feel this function ought to be stressed.

We have been speaking of 'American' students, meaning a sample of
eleven universities representing the main types of universities in the Unite
States. A glance at Table 5.4 will show that there are great variations between universities. It will be seen that the old liberal arts eastern universi
ties such as Wesleyan, Yale, Harvard and Dartmouth stress academic and
humanistic values, general education and appreciation of ideas, while midwestern and southern colleges such as Michigan, Wayne, Texas and Fisk
place more emphasis on instrumental and vocational values. University of
Oslo students are more like students at midwestern and southern universities, but place even greater emphasis on pragmatic and vocational training
values than do any of the eleven American universities studied.

Are the results due to the fact that Norwegian students are somewhat
older and that there are only men in the American sample? The American
research shows that upperclassmen are more oriented toward academic
values and less to vocational ones than are younger students. [7] Thus, if
greater proportions of older American students had been included in the
American sample the proportions of those choosing basic general education
and appreciation of ideas would most probably have been greater than is
shown for the present sample of American students.

It is well known that in the United States women tend to favor the more
humanistic scholarly approaches. Is the same tendency true of Norwegian
students? We tested this hypothesis by controlling for sex. The results are
indicated in Tables 5.5 and 5.6. Differences between men and women are
small and whatever divergences there are between the sexes in this regard
are not statistically significant; we may therefore conclude that differences
between Norwegian and American students are not due to the variable of
sexual social roles.

The conclusion must be that Norwegian students to a greater extent than
American students regard as the chief functions of the university to provide
vocational training and to develop skills and techniques directly applicable t
their careers.

Norwegian students are probably a much more selected group than Ame
cans and come to the university with fairly well-defined purposes. Apparen

7. Goldsen et al., op.cit., pp. 7-13.

Table 5.4. Educational goals stressed* by cross-section of students at each campus polled (percentages)**

Consider what educational goals you think the ideal college or university ought to emphasize	Wes-leyan (277)	Yale (297)	Har-vard (453)	Dart-mouth (365)	Cor-nell Men (655)	North Caro-lina (414)	UCLA (467)	Michi-gan (488)	Texas (516)	Wayne (519)	Oslo (408)	Fisk (134)
Provide a basic general education and appreciation of ideas.	90	88	85	84	73	74	70	69	65	64	60	59
Provide vocational training, develop skills and techniques directly applicable to your career.	36	31	30	32	62	65	68	66	67	74	85	80
Develop your ability to get along with different kinds of people.	76	69	59	75	74	77	64	72	75	70	19	66
Develop your knowledge and interest in community and world problems.	58	57	55	67	48	49	49	47	45	47	42	57
Help develop your moral capacities, ethical standards and values.	60	51	48	45	44	53	41	42	45	44	35	52
Prepare you for a happy marriage and family life.	18	19	11	18	20	27	24	19	24	24	3	28

* Those who marked a goal as being highly (H) important, i.e. the highest as well as 'other' high rankings. (See Questionnaire, Appendix B.)

** Data for American students from Goldsen et al., op.cit., p. 208.

Table 5.5. Ranking of college educational goals by Norwegian men
(n = 281)

Educational goals (items 11 - 22)	Highly important				
	First	Other high	Medium	Low	No data
Provide vocational training and develop skills and techniques directly applicable to your career.	62	23	12	3	0
Develop your ability to get along with different kinds of people.	2	15	44	39	0
Provide a basic general education and appreciation of ideas.	24	37	33	6	0
Develop your knowledge of and interest in community and world problems.	3	37	51	9	0
Help develop your moral capacities, ethical standards and values.	7	28	36	28	1
Prepare you for a happy marriage and family life.	1	2	14	82	1

Note: Percentages should be added horizontally.

Table 5.6. Ranking of college educational goals by Norwegian women
(n = 127)

Educational goals (items 11 - 22)	Highly important				
	First	Other high	Medium	Low	No data
Provide vocational training and develop skills and techniques directly applicable to your career.	63	23	14	0	0
Develop your ability to get along with different kinds of people.	3	21	42	33	1
Provide a basic general education and appreciation of ideas.	18	39	37	5	1
Develop your knowledge of and interest in community and world problems.	6	41	44	9	0
Help develop your moral capacities, ethical standards and values.	12	24	36	28	0
Prepare you for a happy marriage and family life.	0	2	12	84	2

Note: Percentages should be added horizontally.

ιe various faculties of Norwegian universities are essentially professional chools.

Both American and Norwegian students believe that what they are learn-ιg in college is very worthwhile; the proportions are 74 and 80 percent re-ιectively. Americans are more satisfied with their system of college edu-ιtion than the Norwegians are with theirs, as can be seen from Table 5.7. ifty-four percent of Americans reject the idea that college education should ε free to everyone who has the necessary ability, while only 15 percent of orwegian students do so. While the majority of the students of both coun-ies reject the proposition that 'College education does more to break down ιlues than to build up ideals,' more Americans than Norwegians accept this ιea (15 as against 7 percent).

ımmary

Both Norwegian and American students think a university's main function ιould be to provide a basis of general education, appreciation of ideas and ιcational training. They differ with regard to the ranking of these functions, ith the Norwegians placing the more instrumental function first, while ιmericans rank the academic humanistic values first.

The idea of a general education as an educational philosophy has not been ιomoted in Norway to the extent that it has in the United States, and it may ε that the relatively limited resources of the country make it imperative to ιe the university very deliberately to prepare key cadres of highly skilled ιdministrators, scientists and professional people to perform the nation's ssential functional roles. It is also possible that Norwegians mentioned the ιore obvious function assuming that the purpose of a general education would ε achieved without deliberately seeking it.

Students of the two countries also differ to the extent that Norwegians ιfinitely reject preparation for marriage and family life and, to a somewhat sser extent, the development of interpersonal skills, as university functions, ιile Americans stress the latter, and even rank it almost as high as the aca-ιmic functions.

To what extent do the values members of society have regarding their ιstitutions of higher learning reflect basic value orientations and general ιlue systems? There seem to be some valid reasons for believing that the

Table 5.7. American and Norwegian students' responses to
statements evaluation college education
(percentages)

Item number and description	Responses	American* (n = 4,830)	Norwegian (n = 408)	C.R
46. Norway (America) has the best system of college education.	Agree	35	4	12.72
	Disagree	23	62	17.02
	Uncertain	41	33	
	No answer	1	1	
47. College education should be free to everyone who has the necessary ability.	Disagree	54	15	16.11
57. College education does more to break down values than to build up ideals.	Agree	15	7	4.37
	Disagree	65	78	5.28
	Uncertain	19	15	
	No answer	1	-	
75. Most of what I am learning in college is very worth-while.	Agree	74	80	

---

*   Data for American students from Goldsen et al., op. cit., pp. 108, 204
    205.

relationship is fairly close. In the first place, since human culture is learn
any society must, if it is to continue its culture and traditions, do so throug
training each generation in its ways and norms. Universities are the trainix
agencies of its teachers and the repositories of old cultural traditions and
forms as well as the places where new knowledge is evolved. They have
roles, therefore, which may seem incompatible, since they must conserve
as well as innovate. But whether the first function is stressed, as in static
societies, or the latter, as in dynamic ones, the institution of higher learni
is the repository of some of society's basic values. Furthermore, in both t
United States and Norway, where egalitarian democracy and the fullest deve
opment of the personalities and potentialities of the individual are highly
valued, the university is regarded as an instrument for the realization of
these goals as well as the vehicle of social mobility within an open class
system.

VI
OCCUPATIONAL VALUES

One of the basic purposes of this research was to compare American and Norwegian basic values as a basis for understanding differences between their social systems. Following Williams,[1] we conceive of values as concepts of the desirable which can be empirically determined by the criterion of choice. If in the process of making choices a person is attracted to some things and rejects others, if he selects certain things or actions and renounces others, he is giving evidence of his values.

Asking students to make choices related to vocation, we believe, is one of the best ways of getting some idea of the basic values in these societies. There are a number of reasons for holding this hypothesis. First, the degree of validity and reliability of attitude questions is related to the degree of involvement of the respondent in a situation of responsibility derived from the respondent's real involvement in the consequences of choice. The selection of an occupation is one of the really big decisions of a person's life. In most cases within these societies it is the paramount factor in determining the pattern of his life. It is in his work that he must find self-fulfillment. His rewards—money and what it will buy of goods and services, as well as social position, and the status and power he will achieve—will in these countries in most instances be determined by his vocation. Vocational choice may mean the difference between spending eight hours a day in a purgatory of dreary monotonous existence or of leading a creative life in the company of the kind of people he enjoys. For the student who is in the process of making a vocational choice the situation is real; he is in a real sense staking his life on his choice.

We believe, too, that students, the intellectual elite of nations, are, to as great an extent as any group and greater than many, those who are sensitive to societal values and those who have effectively internalized them.

---

1. Robin M. Williams, Jr., op. cit., Chap. XI.

The Meaning and Role of Work in the United States and Norway

Furthermore, we believe that in these two cultures there is an especially close connection between values related to work and vocation and the general value systems. Williams points out that 'American culture is marked by a central stress upon personal achievement, especially secular occupational achievement'[2] and that 'the comparatively striking feature of American culture is its tendency to identify standards of personal excellence with competitive occupational achievement,'[3] and '... achievement is still associated with work, and work is still invested with an almost organic complex of ethical values.'[4] He concludes that if distinctive foci of values can be found in this complicated culture of the United States one should look for it in values related to active performance and work.[5]

That the role and meaning of work is especially important in the value system of Norway is supported by our findings. In response to the question: 'What three things or activities in your life do you expect to give you most satisfaction?' the two most chosen activities were career and family. Twenty-eight percent of Americans and 25 percent of Norwegians thought that career would be the most satisfying activity.[6] Since this slight difference is not statistically significant (C.R. 1.2), it would seem that they are alike in this particular evaluation. However, to be sure that sex differences do not alter the conclusion, we controlled for sex with the results shown in Table 6.1. Again, Norwegian and American men are not statistically different (C.R. 1.1) in thinking that career will be one of their most important life satisfactions, second only to family relationships. American men and women are very much alike, but in the Norwegian group twice as large a proportion of Norwegian women students say they will find their most important life satisfactions in their careers and occupations. The difference between Norwegian men and women is significant (C.R. 3.2). Furthermore, 83 percent of American women as against 69 percent of Norwegian women felt that family relationships would constitute their major source of life satisfaction. Since

2. Op. cit., p. 417.

3. Op. cit., p. 418.

4. Op. cit., p. 419.

5. Op. cit., p. 423.

6. See Table 7.1, for a complete ranking of selected life satisfactions.

Table 6.1. Expected most important life satisfactions of men and
women. American* and Norwegian students
(data expressed as percentages)

	Men		Women	
	American	Norwegian	American	Norwegian
Life satisfactions	(n = 2,007)	(n = 281)	(n = 749)	(n = 127)
Your career or occupation	25	28	8	17
Family relationship	62	60	83	69
Leisure-time recreational activities	6	5	2	1
Religious beliefs or activities	3	3	6	8
Participation as citizen in affairs of your community	1	1	1	2
Participation in activities directed toward national or international betterment	1	1	1	3

* Data about American students is taken from Rosenberg, Occupation
and Values, p. 48, Table 25.

this is a significant difference (C.R. 3.7) it is clear that Norwegian women students are more career- and less family-oriented in their values than American women students. It is of considerable social significance that men and women of both countries expect to find their major life satisfactions not in religion, community or international spheres but in the relatively private individualistic and circumscribed areas of the family and the job.

When we asked students about their vocational values, the greater proportion of both groups chose values which are intrinsic to the nature of the job; that is, for them the most important characteristics that an ideal occupation should have were that it would give them an opportunity to use their special abilities and aptitudes or permit them to be creative or original. If the percentages of American and Norwegian students who made these two intrinsic choices are added, the sums are about identical for both groups, 126 (see Table 6.4). And when asked to choose from a number of qualities two which they thought would really get a young man ahead most quickly today, the quality chosen by a large majority of both groups was 'hard work' (see Table 8.3). Williams believes, regarding the American situation, that if distinctive foci of values can be found in that complicated society, one ought to find them in the stress upon work which is a core element in the historic culture;[7] we believe that the same might be said for the Norwegian situation.

While there are, as we have indicated, striking similarities in the general evaluation of work between Norwegians and Americans, there are also some important differences with regard to certain aspects of vocational values. The choices presented, together with percentages of American and Norwegian students selecting each, are given in Table 6.2. We asked the respondents to indicate next to each requirement if they consider it to be of high or medium importance and to mark those they consider to be of little or no importance, irrelevant, or even distasteful, as low. They were also asked to rank the requirements they had marked high in the order of their importance. To facilitate comparisons we have summarized in Table 6.3 all the high and low choices, together with critical ratios of percentage differences between the American and Norwegian students.

While both American and Norwegian students emphasize intrinsic vocational requirements, they differ significantly as to the specifics of these

---

7. Loc. cit., pp. 423, 424.

Table 6.2. Importance of various occupational requirements of
American and Norwegian students (percentages*)

Occupational requirement	American students (n = 2,975**)				Norwegian students (n = 408)			
	Highly important	Medi-um Other	Low		Highly important	Medi-um Other	Low	
	First	high			First	high		
Provide an opportunity to use my special abilities	27	51	20	2	64	32	3	-
Provide me with a chance to earn a good deal of money	10	29	48	13	1	19	53	26
Permit me to be creative and original	10	38	39	13	5	26	40	27
Give me social status and prestige	2	24	53	21	-	8	42	49
Give me an opportunity to work with people rather than things	7	37	36	20	14	37	29	19
Enable me to look forward to a stable secure future	24	37	31	8	5	41	46	7
Leave me relatively free of supervision by others	3	35	48	14	3	26	41	29
Give me a chance to exercise leadership	4	28	53	15	-	9	34	55
Provide me with adventure	1	15	40	44	1	10	34	54
Give me an opportunity to be helpful to others	10	33	44	13	9	40	38	12

* Percentages should be added horizontally. For the Norwegian sample, the 'no response' percentage (never over 2 percent, and in most cases 1 percent) is omitted from the table.

** Data for American students is taken from Goldsen et al., op.cit., p. 27, Table 2-3.

- Indicates less than 1 percent.

requirements. Sixty-four percent of Norwegians and only 27 percent of Americans think that to 'provide an opportunity to use my special abilities' is the most important. On the other hand, Americans to a greater extent tha Norwegians think that the most important requirement of a vocation is to per mit one to be creative and original (10 as against 5 percent).

Americans are more concerned with an opportunity to earn a lot of mon (10 as against 1 percent) and are more attracted to security (24 as against 5 percent) than Norwegian students. But Norwegians to a greater extent re- quire of an ideal vocation that it give them an opportunity to work with peopl These generalizations are confirmed by the reverse side of the coin; that is by their judgments as to which requirements should be considered unimpor- tant or distasteful. It is interesting to note that the requirements valued low by both Americans and Norwegians, but to a significantly greater extent by Norwegians, are: 'give me social status and prestige', 'chance to exercise leadership' and 'provide adventure'. When considering the first two of these it would seem that egalitarianism is even more pronounced in Norway than in the United States and that Norwegians are reluctant to emphasize status and leadership strivings.

The great emphasis in America on money-making has often been noted by foreigners. But money, in the United States, as Williams points out, 'comes to be valued not only for itself and for the goods it will buy, but as symbolic evidence of success and, thereby, of personal worth.'[8] The greate preoccupation of Americans with security probably reflects their greater in- security in a very competitive society and the Norwegians' lesser need for i in a welfare state. The greater emphasis of Norwegians on working with people may reflect the values of a society which has emphasized social wel- fare for more than a generation. Working with people, for the Norwegians, probably means essentially that they would like to work for people in the sen of helping them, as is shown by the responses to this requirement.

Occupational Values — Men and Women

Because of differences in physical characteristics and social role pre- scriptions, we should expect different occupational values for men and wome Do differences between Americans and Norwegians disappear when we contr

8. Loc. cit., p. 421.

Table 6.3. Requirements of ideal occupations. Percentage of American and Norwegian students ranking occupational requirements as of highest or low importance*

Occupational requirements	Highest importance			Low importance		
	American (n = 2,975)	Norwegian (n = 408)	C.R.	American (n = 2,975)	Norwegian (n = 408)	C.R.
Provide an opportunity to use my special abilities	27	64	15.3	2	-	-
Provide me with a chance to earn a good deal of money	10	1	6.0	13	26	7.0
Permit me to be creative and original	10	5	3.2	13	27	7.5
Give me social status and prestige	2	-	-	21	49	12.3
Give me an opportunity to work with people rather than things	7	14	4.9	20	19	-
Enable me to look forward to a stable, secure future	24	5	8.7	8	7	-
Leave me relatively free of supervision by others	3	3	-	14	1	-
Give me a chance to exercise leadership	4	-	-	15	55	19.0
Provide me with adventure	1	1	-	44	54	4.0
Give me an opportunity to be helpful to others	43	49	2.3	13	12	0.5

-    Indicates less than 1 percent or C.R.'s not calculated because of small numbers and differences.

*   Data from Table 6.2.

Table 6.3.1. Highly important occupational values of men and women
chosen by American and Norwegian students
(data given in percentages*)

Values	Men			Women		
	American** (n = 2,008)	Norwegian (n = 281)	C.R.	American** (n = 750)	Norwegian (n = 127)	C.R
Special abilities or aptitudes	78	97	7.4	80	93	3.?
Earn a good deal of money	36	22	4.6	19	14	1.3
Creative and original	49	34	4.7	54	24	6.?
Social status and prestige	25	9	5.9	15	5	3.(
Work with people rather than with things	39	45	1.9	59	64	1.1
Stable secure future	63	46	5.4	51	46	1.(
Free of supervision by others	46	27	5.5	40	30	2.?
Exercise leadership	38	8	3.2	29	9	4.7
Adventure	14	11	-	17	12	-
Opportunity to help others	37	45	2.5	53	57	0.8

---

* Percentages based on number of choices made by indicated number of men and women. Since a respondent could designate more than one value as being highly important the percentages do not add up to 100.

** Data on American students is taken from Rosenberg, Occupation and Values, p. 49, Table 26.

for sex? Are sex role differentials the same in both national groups? Results of the investigation of these questions are given in Table 6.3.1.

Differences between Americans and Norwegians hold up when controlling for sex with regard to these vocational values to which American men, to a greater extent than Norwegian men, are attracted: earn a good deal of money, creativity and originality, social status and prestige, stable and secure future, freedom from supervision by others, and leadership. When we control for sex, a significantly greater proportion of Norwegians stress 'working with people rather than with things' and 'an opportunity to help others'. For men, then, we find no reason to change our generalizations based on the complete sample.

The conclusions must change somewhat when comparing the women students of the two nations. American and Norwegian women are not significantly different in their evaluation of earning money, working with people rather than things, getting a stable and secure future, or having the opportunity to help others as vocational requirements. Otherwise the generalizations, based on the complete sample, hold. Apparently in American, more than in Norwegian society, earning money and worrying about a secure future are to a greater extent masculine concerns, while working with and helping people seem to be less of a vocational value to American than Norwegian men. It will be seen that women of both countries as compared to the men are more strongly attracted to working with people and opportunity to help others, a finding which definitely reflects cultural role definitions which seem to be alike with regard to these particular activities for women. There is a striking difference between American and Norwegian women with regard to the exercise of leadership, with larger proportions of American women, like American men, evaluating this requirement highly. Apparently American women, to a greater extent than Norwegian women, envisage the possibility of leadership roles.

Patterns of Occupational Values

In the study of American students, values related to vocational requirements seem to cluster around three themes: self-expression, involving a chance to exploit one's special abilities and aptitudes, creativity and originality; service, involving an opportunity to work with people and a chance to be helpful to others; and rewards, including emphasis on money, security and prestige. Self-expression values might be said to be intrinsic since they derive from the nature of the occupational activity itself; service values are

Table 6.4. Occupational value clusters:
percent of Norwegian and American students ranking
occupational requirements as high and low

Occupational value	High importance			Low importance		
	American (n = 2,975)	Norwegian (n = 408)	C.R.	American (n = 2,975)	Norwegian (n = 408)	C.R.
Self-expressive:						
'Use my special abilities and aptitudes'	78	96	8.5	2	-	-
'Permit me to be creative and original'	48	31	6.4	13	27	7.4
Service:						
'Work with people rather than things'	44	51	2.6	20	19	-
'Permit me to be helpful to others'	43	49	2.2	13	12	-
Reward:						
'Opportunity to make a lot of money'	39	20	7.5	13	26	6.9
'Opportunity to acquire social prestige'	26	8	7.9	21	49	13.2
'Opportunity to achieve security'	61	46	5.8	14	29	7.8

- Indicates less than 1 percent or C.R.'s not calculated because of slight differences.

people-oriented, while <u>rewards</u> are valued as a consequence of performing work and are in a sense extrinsic to the work process itself. Table 6.4 compares these clusters of occupational requirements by the accumulation of all choices marked highly important. If the percentage figures for self-expression intrinsic values are added, the sums are almost identical for both nationalities, 126 and 127, but for the Norwegians a much larger proportion of students felt that an opportunity to use their special abilities was of critical importance. Norwegians are significantly more service-oriented than are Americans, although not much more so, but for American students extrinsic rewards are more important than for Norwegians since significantly larger proportions of the former group look for vocations that provide a lot of money, social prestige and security. Low responses are consistent with the above generalizations in that if a large percentage of a group rates a value high, a comparatively small proportion of the same group considers the same requirements to be of low importance.

Changes in Occupational Values

Rosenberg points out that Ginzberg and his associates noted a trend toward the abandonment of the more idealistic occupational values and a shift to the more prosaic extrinsic regards in the upper age groups.[9] Rosenberg and his associates, on the other hand, found no such trend at Cornell, but on the contrary a decreasing concern with the extrinsic reward of security and unchanged concern with money and status.[10] Since our Norwegian student sample is somewhat older than the American one, we thought it necessary to investigate this aspect of the problem. We present the results of this study in Table 6.5.

When comparing first- and fourth-year Norwegian students, it is clear that they behave like the Cornell students in that they tend to abandon the <u>extrinsic</u> values of security, money and prestige as they get nearer graduation and increase their regard for <u>intrinsic</u> values of being creative and original. The occupational requirement that they be able to use their abilities and aptitudes remains consistently high throughout the university career. Generalizations regarding American-Norwegian differences derived from

9. Rosenberg, op. cit., p. 67.

10. Ibid., pp. 68, 69.

Table 6.5. Occupational values rated highly important by American
and Norwegian students of various college classes

Occupational values	First year Am. n=1103	Norw. n=31	Second year Am. n=1040	Norw. n=58	Third year Am. n=1181	Norw. n=73	Fourth year and over Am. n=1251	Norw n=23
	Per-cent	Per-cent	Per-cent	Per-cent	Per-cent	Per-cent	Per-cent	Per-cent
C. Creative and original	43	19	45	38	48	23	53	31
A. Use abilities, aptitudes	75	100	76	97	78	97	79	95
F. Security	69	52	63	43	58	55	53	41
B. Earn a good deal of money	41	29	39	26	37	26	37	14
D. Status and prestige	23	10	25	1	26	10	27	6

For the Norwegian group, 7 respondents who did not answer the questions
were omitted.

Table 6.5.1. Critical ratios of percentage difference

Items and percentages compared		C.R.'s
C(A/N 4th year)	53 - 31	6.2
A(A/N 2nd year)	76 - 97	3.7
A(A/N 4th year)	79 - 95	5.8
F(N/N 1st and 4th year)	52 - 41	1.19
F(A/N 4th year)	41 - 53	3.4
B(A/N 3rd year)	26 - 37	1.8
B(A/N 4th year)	14 - 37	6.9
B(N/N 3rd and 4th year)	26 - 14	7.3

analysis of complete samples do not change when we control for the number
of years in the university: Americans to a greater extent than Norwegians in
every year value creativity, security, money, status and prestige, while
Norwegians are mainly concerned with using their abilities and aptitudes.
Except for the Americans' greater concern with creativity, it would seem
that they, more than the Norwegians, tend to view work as an instrumental
value rather than a goal value.

Differential Values of Selected Occupational Groups

One might expect that students heading for different vocations would have
different values which they expect to realize by making a certain vocational
choice. Results of an investigation into this aspect are indicated in Table 6.6.

American business students, as might be expected, stress money values
significantly more than Americans expecting to enter other professions, and
to a significantly greater extent than Norwegian business students. Norwegian
business students lay equal stress on money and creativity but are much less
concerned with an opportunity to help others.

Students of art and related professions, as might be expected, value creativity most, although Americans in this category are not inclined to worry
about an opportunity to help others. Norwegian art students think the opportunity to help others is as important as creativity.

The largest proportion of all medical students of both nations select an
opportunity to help others as a highly important value. The proportion of
American medical students who think it highly important to earn a great deal
of money is significantly higher than their Norwegian counterparts (C.R. 2.5).

Natural science students of both countries stress creativity rather than any
other value, but a larger percentage of Americans do so than Norwegians
(64 as against 44).

Would-be teachers of both countries apparently see as their chief motivation for engaging in this profession the opportunity to be helpful to others
rather than money or creativity, although American students in this category
value creativity to a greater extent than do Norwegians.

It is clear that students of both countries who expect to enter different
vocational fields stress different values. Generally speaking, those who expect to enter professional fields tend to seek intrinsic rather than reward

Table 6.6. Values stressed by Norwegian and American students
who expect to enter selected occupations*

Expected occupation	Chance to earn a great deal of money		Creativity		Opportunity to help others	
	American	Norwegian	American	Norwegian	American	Norwegian
Business, real estate, finance	58	36	36	32	30	14
Art and related professions	49	8	81	54	28	54
Medicine	33	16	34	16	53	67
Science (Natural)	30	25	64	44	30	39
Teaching	17	16	59	29	47	54

Note: Figures are given in percentages of students in each vocation who marked as highly important 'money', 'creativity' and 'opportunity to help others.'

Table 6.7. Ranking of selected occupations
related to occupational values*

Rank	Money		Creativity		Helpfulness	
	American	Norwegian	American	Norwegian	American	Norwegian
1	B	B	A	A	M	M
2	A	S	S	S	T	T
3	M	M	T	B	S	A
4	S	T	B	T	B	S
5	T	A	M	M	A	B

B = Business, A = Art, M = Medicine, S = Science (Natural), T = Teaching
*   Data from Appendix Table A. 4.

values; those who expect to enter medicine and teaching emphasize helpfulness to others, while arts and related professions and natural scientists
stress creativity. These generalizations are true for both countries.

There are some general differences between American and Norwegian
students when controlling for potential vocation. First, there is a greater
tendency for all kinds of American students to stress money-reward values
and for the Norwegian students to reject them. Secondly, all kinds of Norwegian students except for the business students place greater value on the opportunity to help others. Thirdly, American business students, unlike the
Norwegian ones, seem to have accepted American business ideology to the
extent that they seem to believe that they can help others by engaging in
business activity. Finally, all varieties of American students value creativity to a greater extent than Norwegians.

Are the vocations in both countries similarly selective in attracting students with the same types of vocational values such as money, creativity and
helpfulness? In Table 6.7 we have ranked vocations on the basis of the percentages of students in each vocation who chose the indicated value, with the
greater percentage ranked 1. For example, B in row 1 under both 'Amer-
can' and 'Norwegian' columns indicated that a greater percentage of students
who expected to enter business than these who expected to enter any other
vocation chose 'the opportunity to earn a great deal of money' as being a
highly important vocational value. If we compare along rows across the various columns, it is clear that rank 1 is similar for both countries; that is,
potential businessmen as a group value money most, future artists creativity
and would-be doctors helpfulness to others in both countries. Second rankings
are consistent except for American artists who rank money higher than their
Norwegian counterparts, but Norwegian natural scentists rank money higher
than do their American opposite numbers. The rankings are quite similar
in both countries, not varying more than one rank position except in three
cases.

Preferred Occupational Organization

Norwegian men students to a greater extent than Americans prefer independent professions, educational institutions, social agencies and research
institutions, as will be seen from Table 6.8. American men, to a greater

Table 6.8. Type of occupational organization preferred by
American* and Norwegian men and women students

Type of organization	Men			Women		
	American (n = 2,007)	Norwegian (n = 281)	C.R.	American (n = 794)	Norwegian (n = 127)	C.R.
Own business or own firm	15	7	3.6	3	1	-
Own professional office	10	19	4.5	3	13	5.1
Educational institution	9	36	8.2	30	48	4.0
Social agency	2	7	4.9	8	9	-
Research organization**	3	14	8.6	5	12	-
Governmental agency or bureau	8	5	-	5	4	-
Family business or enterprise	6	1	-	3	2	-
Private firm, organization or factory	43	12	10.0	30	11	4.5
Other	3	-	-	-	-	-
Do not expect to work	1	-	-	-	-	-
No data	-	-	-	-	-	-

*   Data for American students are from Rosenberg et al., Occupation and Values, p. 52, Table 29.

** For the American sample this choice was 'other non-profit organizatio

\-   In C.R. columns indicates C.R.'s not calculated because of small numbers or because of slight differences in percentages.

xtent than Norwegian, look forward to working in their own business or in
  private firm or factory. Thus it would appear that Norwegians look for-
ʹard to careers in some type of governmental institution while Americans
ʹisualize their economic functions as taking place primarily in private enter-
ʹrises.

  It is interesting to note that Norwegian men and women are much more
like in their choice of organizational type than are American men and wo-
ʹen. Differences between men and women with reference to educational in-
ʹtitution in percentage points is twenty-one for Americans and twelve for
ʹorwegians, with reference to private firms the difference is thirteen in the
ʹmerican and only one in the Norwegian group. The greater importance of
ʹrivate enterprise and private firms in the American group and of govern-
ʹental activity in Norway is thus reflected in these choices. The independent
ʹrofessions and family enterprises are apparently less popular than big
ʹovernment and big business as the preferred vocational organizations of
ʹtudents of both countries. Does this mean that students are more interested
ʹn security than in individual risks and possibly greater rewards at the cost
ʹf greater insecurity, or are these choices merely a realistic realization
ʹhat small enterprises are diminishing rapidly as large-scale economic and
ʹovernmental associations take over the majority of societal functions?

VII

LIFE SATISFACTIONS AND SUCCESS

Perhaps the characteristic which more than any other separates the moder
world from the old, the underdeveloped from the developed and the simple
from the complex societies is that a variety of values and styles of life ar
open to choice for men and women of modern complex urban societies. Und
lying the students' specific choices are probably the big end goals which th
hope to achieve in their vocations or by activities in community and nation.
In what sectors of life activity do students expect to achieve the greatest s:
isfactions?

We have already seen that they did not expect to find satisfaction in re
gion and that career is an important source of life satisfaction, but what
about other possibilities? In addition to religion and career we asked students to evaluate other sources of life satisfaction: family relationship, le
sure time, recreational activities, participation as citizens in the affairs (
their community and participation in activities directed toward national or
international betterment.

Of all choices, by far the largest proportion of students of both nation:
selected family relationships as the most important source of life satisfaction. We had expected this of Americans, but to find that Norwegians to an
even greater extent than Americans felt this way was a surprise. We had
expected that Norwegians, because of the relative smallness of the country
their great emphasis on social welfare and their demonstrated concern for
and activity in international affairs, would to a greater extent have found
major life satisfaction in participation in community and world affairs.

Norwegians and Americans are remarkably alike in their placement of
career or occupation in second place as well as in their low evaluation of t
other possible sources of the most satisfactions in life, as will be seen fro
Table 7.1.

In his very revealing and stimulating discussion of major value orient:

Table 7.1. Comparison of basic life satisfactions for
American* and Norwegian students (percentages)**

Question: 'What three things or activities in your life do you expect to give you most satis- faction?'	First in importance		Second and third, etc.		Low	
	Amer- ican	Norwe- gian	Amer- ican	Norwe- gian	Amer- ican	Norwe- gian
Career or occupation	28	25	61	65	11	10
Family relationship	55	63	34	31	11	6
Leisure time recrea- tional activities	5	4	52	55	43	41
Religious beliefs or activities	4	5	13	10	83	85
Participation as a citizen in the affairs of your community	1	2	16	21	83	77
Participation in activ- ities directed toward national or international betterment	1	2	11	20	88	78

---

*   Data for American students from Goldsen et al., op.cit., Table 2-1,
      p. 24.

**   Number of Americans: 2,975; Norwegians: 407.

tions in America, the first prominent American value theme that Williams chooses to discuss is achievement and success.[1] He finds that the American culture hero is characterized by success in overcoming handicaps and diffi- culties in a relentless yet morally disciplined drive to achieve wealth, power status and mastery over nature, as evidence of achievement and ego grati- fication. Is the drive for success particularly American? Are not peoples of all societies eager for it? To answer such questions cross-cultural data are required and we attempted to supply some by asking the Norwegian stu- dents the same questions bearing on this problem as had been asked of the American students.

The first of these questions was: 'If you had your choice, which of the following would you most like to be: independent, successful or well-liked?' Thirty-six percent of Americans and only 17 percent of Norwegians chose 'successful'. Norwegians, on the other hand, would rather be 'independent, as indicated by the fact that 55 percent of this group made that choice while only 24 percent of Americans did so. Americans also, to a greater extent than Norwegians, chose to be 'well-liked.' All differences are significant beyond the 1 percent level of confidence.

The relative position of American and Norwegian students on this ques- tion seems to be supported by answers to this question: 'How important to you personally is it to get ahead in life?'

It will be seen that a significantly larger proportion of Americans think is very important, and that a significantly larger proportion of Norwegians think it unimportant. It seems quite apparent that Americans, as compared to Norwegians, are more concerned with success. One might speculate as to why this is so. Does life in a welfare state blunt the spur of competition or does the society with greater economic controls and more social security dull the appetite for achievement? Or are there certain personality require- ments of Norwegians, for example the desire for independence, that overrid their need for success? We shall leave these conclusions as questions, in- dicating tendencies that should be confirmed by additional evidence.

---

1. Williams, op. cit. , pp. 417-421.

Table 7.2. American and Norwegian students' responses to the
question: 'How important to you, personally, is it to get ahead in life?'

Response	American* (n = 2,975)	Norwegian (n = 408)	C.R.
Very important	59	18	15.6
Fairly important	34	55	8.2
Unimportant	6	22	11.0
Very unimportant	1	3	-
No data	-	1	-

---

* Data for American students from Goldsen et al., op. cit., p. 21.

VIII

SOME BASIC VALUE ORIENTATIONS, ATTITUDES AND BELIEFS

Certain generalized attitudes and values are of general and basic importanc
We shall consider three basic orientations: <u>anomie-alienation</u>, <u>self-other</u>
titudes and beliefs about <u>human nature</u>, which psychologists and sociologist
have found to be useful in accounting for attitudes and behavior in a wide variety of life situations. [1]

Anomie and Alienation

Social theorists since Durkheim have held that anomie and alienation in
crease as societies become bigger and more urbanized, complex and hetero
geneous. As one passes from the small, highly integrated community with
strong personal and kinship ties and well-defined mores, to one of conflicti
heterogeneous values, anonymity, rapid change and tenuous and instrument
social relations, anomie — feelings of impotence in the face of controlling
powers, purposelessness, loneliness, isolation and alienation from vital so
cial institutions — is said to increase. Anomie is closely related to disorga-
nization because the participants in the social system are not motivated to
perform their roles in the absence of stable norms, vital values, meaningful goals and effective behavior. Anomie and alienation exist to a greater o
lesser degree in all societies, and a small amount is probably good, but wi
spread anomie may destroy a society.

One might expect that a comparatively small and relatively culturally
homogeneous society with well-defined norms should evidence less anomie
then the large and diversified society of the United States. We sought to tes
this hypothesis by asking students if they agreed or disagreed with a series
of statements touching various aspects of anomie. One, 'There is little use

1.   Theodore M. Newcomb, Social Psychology. New York: Dryden, 1950,
     Ch. 11; and Morris Rosenberg et al., op. cit.

n writing to public officials,' sought to elicit the amount of feelings of power-essness in the face of distant power figures in a complex governmental ma-hinery. Another, 'It seems almost everything these days is a racket,' tried o determine general faith in the integrity of social institutions. The state-nent 'Often when I am with people I feel lonely' tried to get at the extent to /hich a person feels isolated and alienated. Meaningfulness and purposeful-ess were tested by responses to the proposition: 'Since life is so short, we night as well eat, drink and be merry.' Another symptom of alienation is the eeling that a person cannot achieve a meaningful and satisfactory place in ociety; we plumbed for the presence of this attitude by the statement: These days I often find myself giving up hope of amounting to anything.'

American and Norwegian students' responses to these statements are iven in Table 8.1. It is noteworthy that a much greater proportion of the tudents of both countries reply in most cases to these statements in a man-er which indicates the absence of anomie. On the other hand, about one uarter of the students of both countries reply to the first two questions in a nanner indicating some anomic tendencies.

What is most surprising is that on every indicator, except one, Norwe-;ians have significantly greater tendencies toward anomie than do Americans. 'his differential tendency holds not only for American students as a group, ut also when comparison is made with each of the eleven universities in the Jnited States, as can be seen by analysis of Table 8.2. Only black students rom Fisk University indicate as much alienation as University of Oslo stu-lents. Could it be that to be alienated is a prescribed cultural role for Nor-/egian students? How can such a finding be explained? Why should Norwe-;ian students feel more alienated than Americans? Replies to questions 78 .nd 80, where differences between Americans and Norwegians are large, vould suggest that Norwegians have less confidence in themselves and have nore tenuous personal social relations. We shall follow this lead in the next ;ection by investigating whether Norwegian and American students differ in he way they relate themselves to others.

Table 8.1. Responses to alienation statements.

American and Norwegian students (data given in percentages)

Item number and description		American* (n = 4,830)	Norwegian (n = 408)	C.R
71. There is little use in	Disagree	57.0	49	3.
writing to public officials	Agree	26.2	29	1.:
	Uncertain	15.9	21	-
	No answer	0.7	1	-
77. It seems almost everything	Disagree	68.2	41	11.:
these days is a racket	Agree	24.3	38	6.:
	Uncertain	8.9	20	-
	No answer	0.5	1	-
78. Often when I am with	Disagree	83.6	63	12.:
people I feel lonely	Agree	10.7	29	10.:
	Uncertain	5.0	7	-
	No answer	0.7	1	-
79. Since life is so short we	Disagree	86.7	67	10.:
might as well eat, drink	Agree	7.0	19	8.:
and be merry	Uncertain	5.3	14	-
	No answer	0.9	-	-
80. These days I often find	Disagree	89.3	66	11.:
myself giving up hope	Agree	5.7	23	20.:
of amounting to anything**	Uncertain	5.0	11	-
	No answer	-	-	-
81. No one is going to care	Disagree	62.9	77	7.:
much what happens to	Agree	29.4	14	12.:
you when you get right	Uncertain	7.4	8	-
down to it**	No answer	-	1	-

---

*   Data for American students calculated from Goldsen et al., op.cit.,
Appendix Table 21, p. 227.

** Asked only of Cornell students (n = 900).

Self-Other Attitudes

Value judgments and choices of alternatives are influenced by basic personality tendencies as well as social structure. The explanation of why persons in one society should have greater anomic tendencies than those from another, more complex one may thus be traced to basic personality tendencies rather than to structural differences. Psychologists have noted a relationship between self-other attitudes and people's value systems. Rosenberg illustrates this type of finding by the hypothesis that if an individual tends to have a strong need for affective ties to others for warmth and affection, then he will be attracted to social and work situations where such needs can be met. He points out that Horney has observed that an individual may relate himself to others in three basic ways: 'he may "move toward," "move against," or "move away" from people.'[2] The 'moving away' type seeks to maintain a distance between himself and people and may be called the de-tached personality type; the 'moving toward' type needs the approval, support and affectional response of others. David Riesman's term 'other-directed' might also be used to characterize this type because such a person is motivated chiefly by the desire for social acceptance and approval.[3] It would seem then that an important component of personality is the attachment-detachment dimension, and if we think in terms of ideal types placed in polar positions most persons would fall somewhere in between on an attachment-detachment continuum. Our hypothesis is that Norwegians, relative to Americans, fall nearer the detachment pole while Americans have greater tendencies toward other-directedness or the attachment pole.

To test this hypothesis we asked a number of questions which would give some indication of the relative placement of the two student groups on the attachment-detachment continuum. These questions, together with the students' replies, are reproduced in Table 8.3. A study of this Table shows that Norwegian students, as compared to Americans, on every indicator make replies which show detachment rather than attachment tendencies. To a greater extent than Americans they are less concerned with being well-liked; they value hard work rather than personality; they want to be inde-

---

2. Rosenberg, op. cit., p. 41.

3. David Riesman, in collaboration with Reuel Denney and Nathan Glazer, The Lonely Crowd. New Haven: Yale University Press, 1950.

Table 8.2. Responses indicating alienation and anomie in University of Oslo and eleven American universities* (data given as percentages)

Item number and description	Response	Oslo (n=408)	Fisk (n=134)	North Carolina (n=414)	Texas (n=516)	Yale (n=297)	Wayne (n=519)	Harvard (n=453)	Cornell Men (n=655)	Cornell Women (n=245)	UCLA (n=467)	Dartmouth (n=365)	Michigan (n=488)	Wesleyan (n=277)
71. There is little use in writing to public officials	Disagree	49	33	48	52	54	58	58	59	60	60	61	63	63
	Agree	29	39	36	33	27	25	22	25	20	25	23	24	20
	Uncertain	21	25	13	14	18	17	19	16	20	14	14	13	17
	No answer	1	3	2	-	1	1	1	-	-	1	1	-	-
77. It seems almost everything these days is a racket	Disagree	41	31	58	59	70	62	75	70	69	63	69	72	78
	Agree	38	49	33	33	24	29	15	20	19	25	21	21	14
	Uncertain	20	16	7	7	6	9	10	10	13	11	9	7	7
	No answer	1	4	2	-	-	1	-	-	-	1	1	-	-
78. Often when I am with people I feel lonely	Disagree	63	78	81	83	81	84	78	86	82	86	87	85	88
	Agree	29	15	13	12	14	12	15	9	9	9	7	9	6
	Uncertain	7	3	4	5	5	3	6	5	9	4	5	6	6
	No answer	-	3	3	-	-	1	1	-	-	1	1	-	-
79. Since life is so short we might as well eat, drink and be merry	Disagree	67	83	84	85	87	86	88	87	89	85	84	91	91
	Agree	19	7	8	10	6	7	6	7	5	8	7	6	5
	Uncertain	14	7	5	5	6	5	5	6	6	6	8	3	3
	No answer	-	3	3	-	1	2	1	-	-	1	-	-	-
80. These days I often find myself giving up hope of amounting to anything**	Disagree	66							91	85				
	Agree	23							4	10				
	Uncertain	11							5	5				
	No answer	--							-	-				
81. No one is going to care much what happens to you when you get right down to it**	Disagree	77							64	60				
	Agree	14							28	34				
	Uncertain	8							8	6				
	No answer	1							-	-				

* Data for American students from Goldsen et al., op. cit., Appendix Table 21, p. 227.

** Asked only of Cornell and Norwegian students.

pendent rather than well-liked; they do not find it as easy to make friends; they expect people to look out for themselves rather than help others; and, as can be seen from the previous Table (Table 8.2), a significantly greater proportion of them say that they often feel lonely when they are with people. It would seem probable, therefore, that the greater feeling of alienation of Norwegian students stems from their basic orientation of detachment in their relations with others. Persons characterized by detachment tend to stress principles rather than human relations and impersonal values rather than personal ones.

Faith in Human Nature

The conclusion that Norwegians seek detachment to a greater extent than Americans is strengthened by a comparison of the two national groups' concepts of the nature of human nature. The questions are from Rosenthal's Faith-in-Human-Nature Scale whose validity has been tested to a considerable extent in the United States by empirical research. [4] Some of these items shown in Table 8.4 could also be considered as a test of the attachment-detachment hypothesis, particularly items 83, 'Human nature is fundamentally cooperative,' and 88, 'Would you say that most people are inclined to help others or to look out for themselves?' Differences between American and Norwegian students' answers to the latter statement are particularly striking, with 26 percent of Americans and only 7 percent of Norwegians saying that most people are inclined to help others, while 72 percent of Americans and 92 percent of Norwegians thought most people were inclined to look out for themselves.

With regard to faith in human nature, it would seem that American students show greater faith in human nature in three out of five statements. However we question the validity of the scale in Norway since item 88, within the Norwegian cultural frame of reference, has little to do with faith in human nature, but everything to do with the cultural norm and value of self-sufficiency. A paramount Norwegian value related to personal characteristics is self-sufficiency; thus the Norwegian students are in effect only stating

4. The reproducibility of the scale was 0.92. Statements included on the scale are indicated by asterisks. Rosenthal et al., op.cit., p. 26. See also Ch. III in this work and Goldsen et al., op.cit., pp. 139, 149-152, 190-192, 135-139, 187-195 for validating data.

Table 8.3. Comparison of American and Norwegian students
on indications of other-directedness (percentages)

Item number and question	Response	American* (n = 2,975)	Norwegian (n = 408)	C.R
94. How important is it for you to be well-liked by different kinds of people?	Very important	37	11	10.
	Fairly important	47	52	-
	Fairly unimportant	13	32	9.
	Very unimportant	3	5	-
43.-44. What two qualities on this list do you think really get a young person ahead the fastest today?**	Having a pleasant personality	57	22	12.
	Hard work	62	76	5.
	Brains	31	75	-
	Knowing the right people^{+}	32	22^{+}	-
	Good luck	5	7	-
	Being a good politician	5	16	-
45. If you had your choice, which of the following would you most like to be?***	Independent	24	55	12.
	Successful	36	17	7.
	Well liked	39	28	4.
93. Would you say you are the sort of person who finds it easier or harder to make friends than most people?***	Easier	39	22	6.
	About the same	49	67	-
	Harder	12	11	-

* Data for American students from Goldsen et al., op. cit., p. 18.

** Percentages should not be cumulated owing to multiple responses.

*** Asked of Cornell students only (n = 1,571),
from Goldsen et al., loc. cit.

$^{+}$ This choice for the Norwegian data was 'Consideration'.

Table 8.4. Comparison of American and Norwegian students
regarding faith in human nature (percentages)

Item number and description		American* (n = 2,975)	Norwegian (n = 408)	C.R.
31. No one is going to care much what happens to you when you get right down to it	Agree	31	14	7.1
	Disagree	60	77	6.6
	Uncertain	9	8	-
	No answer	-	1	-
32. If you don't watch yourself people will take advantage of you	Agree	60	38	8.4
	Disagree	28	41	5.4
	Uncertain	11	20	-
	No answer	1	1	-
33. Human nature is fundamentally co-operative	Agree	68	54	5.6
	Disagree	18	20	-
	Uncertain	14	26	-
	No answer	-	-	-
37. Some people say that most people can be trusted. Others say you can't be too careful in your dealings with people. How do you feel about it?	Most people can be trusted	81	76	2.4
	You can't be too careful	19	22	1.4
	No answer	-	2	-
38. Would you say that most people are inclined to help others or to look out for themselves?	Help others	26	7	8.4
	Look out for themselves	72	92	8.6
	No answer	2	1	-

* Data for American students from Goldsen et al., op.cit., Table 17, p. 221.

what the norm of the society is. That something besides faith in human nature is contaminating the unidimensionality of the scale in Norway is indicated by the fact that its reproducibility for the Norwegian sample is only 74.2. The additional dimensions besides faith in human nature that these statements seem to reflect are therefore probably attachment-detachment attitudes and self-sufficiency values.

IX
SUMMARY AND CONCLUSIONS

The interpretation of responses to similar questions asked of two sets of respondents socialized in different cultural environments presents difficulties, and one must be constantly aware of the problems involved. We therefore used trained sociologists who were completely familiar with both cultures as translators. The interpretation of results similarly had to be done by someone familiar with both cultures. I have studied Norwegian and American cultures for many years and have had many years of residence in each country.

But the effects of different cultural frames of reference are hard to avoid no matter what one does, and particularly if true comparability is another requirement of the research effort. The difficulties we experienced in achieving satisfactory reproducibility coefficients in Guttman-type scale analysis indicates that responses to individual questions are not always hooked up in the same combinations of factors in the two societies.

Similarities between American and Norwegian Students

Political students of both countries tend to conservatism, as interpreted within the ideological frame of reference of their respective countries. In fact, on some questions Norwegians are more conservative than American students from the most conservative of the universities studied, Texas and North Carolina.

Both sets of students apparently feel a need for some 'religious' faith and philosophy, but apparently find that the traditional religions do not give it to them. They are not, therefore, committed to a religious way of life and do not expect religion to be a source of major life satisfaction to them. What religion they have seems to be secular in character.

Students from both countries are strong in their beliefs in humanistic and pacifistic principles, but Americans in particular find it difficult to maintain them when faced with the dilemma presented by the harsh realities of the cold war. Both groups, however, are optimistic about efforts to prevent war.

Students from both countries consider that both vocational training and general education should be emphasized in college education, and relegate to residual values to be achieved by a university education the development of knowledge, interest in community and world problems and the furthering of ethical and moral standards. Both Americans and Norwegians believe that what they are learning in college is worthwhile and the majority of both groups reject the idea that college education does more to break down values than to build up ideals.

Norwegian and American students place hard work and careers high in their value hierarchy, and both groups choose vocational values which are intrinsic to the nature of the work. As they mature, students of both countries tend to put higher value on intrinsic vocational rewards rather than on reward values such as money and prestige. The occupational requirement that they be able to use their abilities and aptitudes remains consistently high throughout the university career.

Students aiming at different vocations evidence different value orientations. In both countries, business students stress money, art students and scientists, creativity, and medical and educational students want their jobs to give them an opportunity to help others.

Family relationships was selected as the most important source of life satisfaction, and career was placed second, while both groups placed leisure-time activity, religious activity and participation in community, national and international affairs far down the list of activities from which they expected to get their major life satisfactions.

Feelings of alienation and anomie are supposed to be characteristic of modern societies, but greater proportions of both sets of respondents replied to questions in a manner which indicates that as far as they are concerned anomie and alienation are not problems.

Differences between Norwegians and Americans

While Norwegian and American students are conservative within their respective countries, Norwegians are much more to the left when questioned n the same issues to which American students responded, except for wo striking examples. Greater proportions of students at the Universi-y of Oslo take a conservative position on questions relating to a minimum wage and the effect of a welfare state on initiative than do students of the most conservative colleges in the United States.

On all indices of religiousness, as here defined, Americans were more religious than Norwegians, and Norwegians had the greater proportion of atheists among them.

Norwegian students are strongly and consistently pacifist, while the majority of Americans, though pacifist in their abhorrence of war, would accept the necessity of engaging in one to defend themselves against Communism.

Contrary to our expectations, Norwegian students, to a greater degree than Americans, when questioned on the functions of a university, took the pragmatic, utilitarian view that the function of a university should primarily be to provide vocational training and to develop skills and techniques direct-ly applicable to their careers. Significantly larger proportions of Ameri-cans took the idealistic position that a university should stress general edu-cation and the development of an appreciation of ideas.

The widely held stereotype that Americans are more pragmatic, utili-tarian and instrumental, and that Europeans are more concerned with human-istic scholarship and general education, must therefore be rejected as far as Norwegian students are concerned. Norwegians definitely reject prepara-tion for family life and the development of interpersonal skills as university functions, while Americans do so to a lesser degree.

It would seem that the stress on work is a core element in both cultures and both emphasize intrinsic vocational requirements, but larger propor-tions of Norwegians than Americans are concerned with being able to use their special abilities in a job, while Americans stress creativity and originality.

Norwegians generally are significantly more service-oriented than Americans. Apparently in American more than in Norwegian society earn-ing money and worrying about a secure future are to a greater extent mascu-line concerns, while working with and helping people seems to be reserved for the ladies. A striking difference between American and Norwegian wo-men in their role concepts is that Americans aspire to the exercise of leadership in their vocation to a greater extent than do the Norwegian women.

With regard to the preferred occupational type of organization, both Norwegian men and women to a greater extent than Americans prefer independent professions, educational institutions, social agencies and research institutions while Americans look forward to working in their own business or in a private firm or factory. The greater impact of government and welfare activity in Norway and the preponderant role of private business enterprise in America seem to be reflected in the students' preferences.

It was somewhat unexpected that Norwegians, who seem so state-welfare and internationally oriented, should to a greater extent than Americans say that they expected to find most of their life satisfaction in the privacy of family life rather than in community, national and international affairs. It was not unexpected that Americans would, to a much greater extent than Norwegians, stress the importance of success and getting ahead in life.

We expected that students of a comparatively small and relatively homogeneous society such as Norway would evidence less anomie and alienation than the large heterogeneous society of the United States, but we found that on every indicator here used, except one, Norwegian students have significantly greater tendencies to alienation than do Americans. However, additional analysis indicates that the alienation may be a function of the Norwegian's detachment, for Norwegians on every one of our indicators, when compared with Americans, show detachment rather than attachment personality tendencies, that is, they value hard work rather than personality, they want to be independent rather than well-liked, they do not find it as easy as Americans to make friends and they expect people to look out for themselves rather than help others. Some people characterized by detachment tend to stress principles rather than human relations and impersonal values rather than personal ones. The Norwegian's great concern for social welfare and social justice may thus be motivated by a greater attachment to moralistic principles than a concern for people.

We have studied the values and beliefs of Norwegian and American students and have found them alike in many ways, but they also differ in many crucial respects. To what extent do students' attitudes and values reflect those of the larger society of which their group is a small part?

We should recognize that Norwegian students, because of their partic-
lar role in society, may be somewhat atypical in their opinions relating
o certain aspects of the value system. It is something of a tradition for
Iorwegian students to be unorthodox in their views and to act as loyal and
ociferous opposition to whomever and whatever represent s the establish-
ient or the surrogates of power and authority. Their relative conserva-
ism in politics, as seen within the Norwegian frame of reference, and their
adicalism in religious matters, might be interpreted as a protest stance
gainst the Labor Party, which was in power at the time, and the State Luthe-
an Church whose doctrines they have been forced to study for years. On
he other hand, the Conservative Party was strong in Norway and conserva-
ive tendencies were gaining in 1962-1963, particularly within the Labor
'arty; and, though Norway has strong, quite fundamentalist religious groups,
he majority of Norwegians are probably less religious than Americans by
vhatever index one uses.

There are undoubtedly differences between students and other groups
1 the society, but it would seem, from the internal evidence and from the
esults of the American investigation, that students do reflect beliefs and
alue tendencies which are compatible with the norms of their society and
1eir subgroups.

Appendix A

Background Data Tables

Table A.1. Occupational aims of Norwegian students

Occupation	No.	Percent
Teaching	200	49.0
Artistic and related fields	3	0.7
Advertising, public relations	1	0.2
Medicine	49	12.0
Law	10	2.5
Natural sciences	36	8.8
Engineering	1	0.2
Social work	10	2.5
Social sciences	6	1.5
Business, real estate, finance	16	3.9
Farming	1	0.2
Sales, promotion	4	1.0
Dentist	10	2.5
Government	11	2.7
Real estate, finance	2	0.5
Journalism	7	1.7
Don't know or no answer	9	2.7
Humanistic, artistic, research	10	2.5
Business administration	4	1.0
No information	18	4.4
Totals	408	100

Table A.2. Income of fathers of Norwegian students

Income	No.	Percent
1. Under 10.000 kroner	30	7.4
2. 10,000 - 14,999	33	8.1
3. 15,000 - 19,999	69	16.9
4. 20,000 - 24,999	68	16.7
5. 25,000 - 29,999	54	13.2
6. 30,000 - 39,999	68	16.7
7. 40,000 and over	54	13.2
8. No data	32	7.8
Totals	408	100.0

Table A.3. Religion of Norwegian students

Religion	No.	Percent
1. Lutheran State Church	320	78.4
2. Other Protestant denominations when specified	9	2.1
3. Catholic	6	1.5
4. Agnostic	2	0.5
5. Atheist	2	0.5
6. None	61	15.0
7. No data	8	2.0
Totals	408	100.0

Table A. 4. Norwegian students' estimation of their own future standard of living relative to that of their family of orientation

Living standards	No.	Percent
1. My living standard will be higher	204	50.0
2. My living standard will be about the same	176	43.1
3. My living standard will be lower	24	5.9
4. No data	4	1.0
Totals	408	100

Table A. 5. Marital status of American and Norwegian students

University	Percentage at each university who are: Married	Single	Total
Oslo	14	85	408
Wayne	24	57	519
Texas	19	64	516
UCLA	13	71	467
Michigan	12	65	488
North Carolina	10	65	414
Fisk	6	65	134
Cornell: Men	5	77	655
Women	1	63	245
Dartmouth	2	78	365
Wesleyan	2	78	277
Yale	2	78	297
Harvard	2	81	453

Note: Percentage not accounted for in American universities are found in a category called 'Engaged, pinned or otherwise going steady' and in the Norwegian sample 1 percent was divorced.

Table A.6. Part of country where Norwegian students lived for most
of their lives

Part of country	No.	Percent
1. Østlandet	208	51.0
2. Vestlandet	92	22.5
3. Sørlandet	32	7.8
4. Trøndelag	33	8.1
5. Nord-Norge	38	9.3
6. Abroad	2	0.5
7. No data	3	0.7
Totals	408	99.9

Table A.7. Description of work of father by Norwegian students

Type of work	No.	Percent
1. Worker	64	15.7
2. White-collar worker in government, business or industry	154	37.7
3. Independent without hired help	83	20.3
4. Independent with hired help	96	23.5
5. No data	11	2.7
Totals	408	99.9

Table A. 8. Distribution of Norwegian student sample by year in
university

Year	No.	Percent
First	32	7. 8
Second	59	14. 5
Third	75	18. 4
Fourth	97	23. 8
Fifth	71	17. 4
Over five	73	17. 5
No data	1	0. 2
Totals	408	99. 6

Table A. 9. Sex of Norwegian student sample

Sex	No.	Percent
Male	281	68. 9
Female	127	31. 1
Totals	408	100. 0

Table A.10. Type of community where Norwegian students grew up

Type of community	No.	Percent
1. Large city	67	16.4
2. Small city	136	33.3
3. Built-up country districts	71	17.4
4. Country	97	23.8
5. Lived in various types of places	37	9.1
Totals	408	100.0

Table A.11. Self placement of class status of families by Norwegian students

Class	No.	Percent
1. Upper class	61	15.0
2. Middle class	286	70.1
3. Lower class	56	13.7
4. No data	5	1.2
Totals	408	100.0

Table A. 12. Occupation of fathers of Norwegian students

Occupation	No.	Percent
Professional	94	23. 0
Managerial business or industry	60	14. 7
Government service managerial	38	9. 3
Government service clerical	3	0. 7
Sales	8	2. 0
Business clerical	17	4. 2
Semi-professional	16	3. 9
Skilled worker, foreman	36	8. 8
Operative	1	0. 2
Unskilled labor - industry, forestry, mines, farms, fishing	23	5. 6
Farmer (owner)	49	12. 0
Small business owner	26	6. 4
No data	36	9. 0
Totals	408	100. 0

Table A.13. Age of Norwegian students

Age	No	Percent
19	10	2.5
20	25	6.1
21	30	7.4
22	66	16.2
23	70	17.2
24	63	15.4
25	35	8.6
26	48	11.8
27	18	4.4
28	14	3.4
29	8	2.0
30	4	1.0
31	5	1.2
32	1	0.2
33	1	0.2
37	1	0.2
45	1	0.2
No data	8	2.0
Totals	408	100.0

Table A.14. Ranking of various occupational requirements by Norwegian student sample

Occupational requirements	Highly important First		Other high		Medium (M)		Low (L)		No data		Totals	
	No.	Per cent	No.	Per cent	No.	Per cent	No.	Per cent	No.	Per cent	No.	Per cent
A. Provide an opportunity to use my special abilities or aptitudes	260	64	130	32	14	3	1	0	3	1	408	100
B. Provide me with a chance to earn a good deal of money	5	1	75	19	217	53	106	26	5	1	408	100
C. Permit me to be creative and original	22	5	104	26	165	40	110	27	7	2	408	100
D. Give me social status and prestige	0	0	31	8	172	42	200	40	5	1	408	100
E. Give me an opportunity to work with people rather than things	56	14	152	37	118	29	78	19	4	1	408	100
F. Enable me to look forward to a stable, secure future	19	5	168	41	187	46	29	7	5	1	408	100
G. Leave me relatively free of supervision by others	11	3	105	26	168	41	120	29	4	1	408	100
H. Give me a chance to exercise leadership	0	0	35	9	138	34	228	55	7	2	408	100
I. Provide me with adventure	4	1	42	10	137	34	220	54	5	1	408	100
J. Give me an opportunity to be helpful to others	37	9	163	40	154	38	50	12	4	1	408	100

Questionnaire in English and Norwegian

STUDENT OPINION QUESTIONNAIRE

'his questionnaire has been answered by students in various American uni-
ersities. The students have told us about the way they see the world they
ive in, what they want out of it and why. They have told us what they think
f some of their major institutions and their beliefs about education, career,
/ork, government, religion and about war and peace.

Dr. Jonassen, a sociologist from the Ohio State University, has come to
Norway as a Fulbright research scholar. He would like to find out what differ-
nces and similarities there may be between Norwegian and American stu-
lents with regard to what they think about these matters.

The United States, like Norway, has a complex division of labor, and
•oth societies therefore have problems of recruiting the right people to fill
. great variety of positions. From an individual's point of view, it is often
lifficult to choose among a large variety of possible vocations that one for
/hich he is best fitted and in which he can make the greatest contribution to
•ociety and best further his own development and self-realization. In answer-
ng these questions you will also help social scientists develop knowledge
vhich will aid counselors and help individuals choose the jobs for which they
.re best fitted. This study may be extended to additional countries and thus
vhatever generalizations may come of of this research will be more valid
or having been based on data from different cultures.

To a Norwegian, the answers to some of these questions may seem self-
evident and perhaps other questions are not altogether applicable to Norwegian
students, but if we are to get true comparability, we must ask the questions
n the same way that they were asked of American students. So please bear
vith us and answer the questions as well as you can.

There are no 'right' answers and students have all kinds of opinions about these matters. Please do not confer with others since we are interes in what <u>you</u> <u>personally</u> believe or feel about the subjects with which these q tions deal.

Your answers will be <u>anonymous</u> and will therefore <u>not</u> be connected wi you or your name. Your answers will be treated merely as items contribut to statistics describing groups and <u>no</u> single individual's opinion or answer will be known.

Institutt for Samfunnsforskning, Oslo
The Ohio State University, Columbus, U.S.A.
Oslo 1962

SOME GENERAL DIRECTIONS FOR THE RESPONDENTS

n this questionnaire the questions are underlined and under each of them
vill be found several possible numbered answers to the questions.
ions.

Please read each question carefully.

Read all the possible answers included under each question.

Each question or set of questions has directions included in parentheses
r underlined. Please read and follow these directions carefully.

Then respond to the question in accordance with the directions given
ither by circling the number of the answer which most nearly applies to you
r corresponds with your opinion, or by supplying the information called for.

If you make a mistake or want to change your mind, cross out the wrong
nswer and supply a new correct one.

It is very important for the outcome of this research that you answer all
questions as frankly and honestly as you can.

When you have completed the questionnaire will you please check and see
hat you have not left out any answers. Thank you.

One of our assistants will contact you within a couple of days to collect
he completed questionnaire.

Thank you very much for your help.

4. If you could have a choice in the matter what kind of firm or outfit would you LIKE BEST to work in after you finish your schooling?

(Circle only the one you would like best.)

1. Own business or own farm
2. Own professional office
3. Educational institution
4. Social agency
5. Other non-profit organization
6. Government bureau or agency
7. Military service
8. Family business or enterprise
9. Private firm, organization, factory
10. Other: (Specify) _____

5-10. What three things or activities in your life do you expect to give you the most satisfaction?

(Please write 1 in the space preceding the most important, 2 in the space preceding next most important, 3 in the space preceding third most important

Career or occupation

Family relationships

Leisure-time recreational activities

Religious beliefs or activities

Participation as citizen in affairs of the community

Participation in activities directed toward national or international betterment

11-22. College students have different ideas about the main purposes of college education. Some of their ideas are listed below. As you read this list, consider what educational goals you think the ideal college or university ought to emphasize. Indicate your opinion by writing:

H (high) next to the goals you consider highly important in a university
M (medium) next to the goals you consider of medium importance
L (low) next to the goals you consider of little importance, irrelevant, or even distasteful to you (Indicate H, M, L,)

a. Provide vocational training; develop skills and techniques directly applicable to your career.

b. Develop your ability to get along with different kinds of people.

c. Provide a basic general education and appreciation of ideas.

d. Develop your knowledge and interest in community and world problems.

e. Help develop your moral capacities, ethical standards and values.

f. Prepare you for a happy marriage and family life.

Now go back and rank the ones you rated H by writing next to each H:

1   for the most important
2   for the second most important

and so on for all the Hs on your list. Do not rank the Ms and Ls.

23-42. When they reported their requirements for an ideal job or profession students said it would have to satisfy certain requirements. Some of these

quirements are listed below. As you read the list, consider to what ex-
nt a job or career would have to satisfy each of these requirements before
u could consider it <u>ideal.</u>

Indicate your opinion by writing:

H (high) next to the requirements you consider highly important

M (medium) next to the requirements you consider of medium importance

L (low) next to the requirments you consider of little or no importance,
irrelevant, or even distasteful to you.

he ideal job for me would have to ... (indicate H, M, L)

a. Provide me with an opportunity to use my special abilities or
aptitudes.

b. Provide me with a chance to earn a good deal of money.

c. Permit me to be creative and original.

d. Give me social status and prestige.

e. Give me an opportunity to work with people rather than things.

f. Enable me to look forward to a stable, secure future.

g. Leave me relatively free of supervision by others.

h. Give me a chance to exercise leadership.

i. Provide me with adventure.

j. Give me an opportunity to be helpful to others.

ow go back and look at the requirements you rated high. Rank them in the
rder of importance to you by writing next to each H:

1 for the most important

2 for the next in importance

nd so on, for all the Hs on your list. Do <u>not</u> rank the Ms and Ls.

3-44. <u>What TWO qualities on this
ist do you think really get a young
erson ahead fastest today?</u>

Circle only <u>two</u>)

1. Hard work
2. Pleasant personality
3. Brains
4. Consideration of others
5. Good luck
6. Being a good politician

45. <u>If you had your desire, which of
the following would you MOST like to
be?</u>

(Circle only <u>one</u>)

1. Independent
2. Successful
3. Well-liked

Do you agree or disagree with the following statements?

(Circle the A if you agree, the D if you disagree, and the ? if you are not sure or have no opinion)

46. Norway has the best system of college education .... A D ?

47. College education should be free to everyone who has the necessary ability .... A D ?

48. The best government is the one which governs least .... A D ?

49. Labor unions in this country are doing a fine job .... A D ?

50. Government planning almost inevitably results in the loss of individual liberties and freedom......................... A D ?

51. Social justice can be achieved only in a socialist country .... A D ?

52. If people are certain of a minimum wage they might lose their initiative .... A D ?

53. The individual employer should sacrifice the privilege of hiring and firing without restriction for the social welfare ..... A D ?

54. The welfare state tends to destroy individual initiative........ A D ?

55. Obedience and respect for authority are the most important truths children should learn .... A D ?

56. Democracy depends fundamentally on the existence of free business enterprise .... A D ?

57. College education does more to break down values than to build up ideals .... A D ?

58. The laws governing labor unions are not strict enough .... A D ?

59. In spite of all our efforts for peace, nations just can't live together peacefully so we might as well expect a war every few years... A D ?

60. If there is no ceiling on business profits there is a better chance to develop products at lower cost .... A D ?

61. Human lives are too important to be sacrificed for the preservation of any form of government .... A D ?

62. A nation's rights are determined by that nation's power........ A D ?

63. A society should guarantee everyone an acceptable standard of living... A D ?

64. Persons who agitate for peace are mostly irresponsible idealists .... A D ?

65. Peace and war are both essential to progress .... A D ?

66. Political representatives are usually pawns in the hands of special interests .... A D ?

67. I regard the church as a harmful institution breeding narrow-mindedness, fanaticism and intolerance .... A D ?

68. I feel the church is a very important agency for inspiration in the world .... A D ?

69. I feel I need to believe in some sort of religious faith or philosophy .... A D ?

70. My religious group has its own personality - something over and above the individual member in it .... A D ?

71. There is little use writing to public officials because often they aren't really interested in the problems of the average man .... A D ?

72. The general public is not qualified to vote on today's complex issues .... A D ?

73. Political candidates are usually run by political machines ...... A D ?

74. I think that university teachers are afraid to say what they really believe these days .... A D ?

75. Most of what I am learning at the university is very worthwhile .... A D ?

76. I feel I now have an adequate faith or philosophy as a guide to my conduct .... A D ?

77. It seems almost everything these days is a racket .... A D ?

78. Often when I am with people I feel lonely .... A D ?

79. Since life is so short we might as well eat, drink and be merry.. A D ?

80. These days I often find myself giving up hope of ever amounting to anything .... A D ?

81. No one is going to care much what happens to you when you get right down to it .... A D ?

82. If you don't watch yourself people will take advantage of you .... A D ?

83. Human nature is fundamentally cooperative .... A D ?

84. I usually don't have enough confidence in myself .... A D ?

85. I get upset if someone criticizes me, no matter who it is ..... A D ?

86. In order to get ahead these days you can't afford to be
squeamish about the means you use .... A D ?

(Please circle the number in front of the statement which most nearly represents your opinion or applies to you.)

87. Some people say that most people can be trusted. Others say you can't
be too careful in your dealings with people. How do you feel about it?

    1. Most people can be trusted
    2. You can't be too careful

88. Would you say that most people are inclined to help others or more inclined to look out for themselves?

    1. To help others
    2. To look out for themselves

89. How would you say you feel most of the time - in good spirits or in low
spirits?

    1. Very good spirits   4. Fairly low spirits
    2. Fairly good spirits   5. Very low spirits
    3. Neither good nor bad

90. Are you the sort of person who lets things worry you or don't you let
things worry you?

    1. Let things worry me very much   3. Let things worry me somewhat
    2. Let things worry me quite a bit   4. Don't let things worry me

91. How important to you, personally, is it to get ahead in life?

    1. Very important   3. Not very important
    2. Fairly important   4. Very unimportant

92. Do you ever get as worked up about something that happens in political
or public affairs as you do about something that happens in your personal life?

    1. Yes
    2. No

93. Would you say you are the sort of person who finds it easier or harder
to make friends than most people?

    1. Easier
    2. About the same
    3. Harder

94. How important is it to you for you to be well liked by different kinds of people?

1. Very important   3. Fairly unimportant
2. Fairly important   4. Very unimportant

95. How much does it bother you to be given orders by someone else?

1. It bothers me very much
2. It bothers me a little
3. It doesn't bother me at all

96. How much does it bother you to have to give orders to other people?

1. It bothers my very much
2. It bothers me a little
3. It doesn't bother me at all

97. When you are in a group do you prefer to make decisions yourself, or do you prefer others to make the decisions?

1. Usually prefer to make decisions myself
2. Usually prefer to have others make decisions
3. Not sure which I prefer

98. How important is it for you to know your plans for the future in advance?

1. Very important
2. Fairly important
3. Not very; not at all

99. Which do you think is the best way for a nation to conduct rocket and space experiments?

1. Conduct experiments as much as possible in secret and tell about them only when and if they have been successful.
2. Conduct all experiments in the open with full publicity thus exposing both failures and successes.
3. One way is as good as another.

100. Which do you personally count as the more effective deterrent against war?

1. The atom bomb
2. The United Nations

101. Do you think it would be worth fighting an all-out war to stop communism, or not? (Please circle one)

1. Very worthwhile   4. Hardly worthwhile
2. Fairly worthwhile   5. Not at all worthwhile
3. Undecided   6. No answer

102. Which ONE of the following statements most closely describes your ideas about the Deity? (Please circle the number before the statement which most nearly describes your belief.)

1. I believe in a Divine God, Creator of the Universe, who knows my innermost thoughts and feelings, and to whom one day I shall be accountable.
2. I believe in a power greater than myself, which some people call God and some people call Nature.
3. I believe in the worth of humanity but not in God or a Supreme Being.
4. I believe in Natural Law, and that the so-called universal mysterie are ultimately knowable using scientific methods.
5. I am not quite sure what I believe.
6. I am an atheist.

(Please circle the number before the choice which applies to you, or fill in the indicated information in the space provided.)

103. In what school (faculty) are you enrolled?

1. Theology   3. Medicine   5. Natural Sciences
2. Law   4. Liberal Arts 6. Dentistry

104. What is your major subject?

105. What occupation do you expect to follow?

106. Year in the University: 1st; 2nd; 3rd; 4th; 5th; other

107. How many years have you studied English?

108. Age on last birthday

109. Sex: 1. Male   2. Female

110. Marital status: 1. Single   3. Divorced
                          2. Married   4. Widow (Widower)

111. In what kind of place did you grow up?

1. Big city   4. Rural area
2. Small city   5. Lived at times in all
3. Fairly densely populated   of these before 21 yrs.
   rural area   of age.

112. What is your commune?

113. In which region of the country have you lived most of your life?

1. Østlandet   3. Sørlandet   5. Nord-Norge   7. Other
2. Vestlandet   4. Trøndelag   6. Foreign Country

114. What is your religion?

115. In which of these three groups do you consider your family to be? (Please circle one)

    1. Upper class
    2. Middle class
    3. Working class (Arbeider)

116. Which political party do you feel most nearly represents your views with regard to political matters?

    1. Labor   3. Communist   5. Conservative   7. Liberal
    2. Center   4. Socialist   6. Christian   8. None of these
                                                      9. Don't know

117. Which political party do you think most nearly represents your father's views with regard to political matters?

    1. Labor   3. Communist   5. Conservative   7. Liberal
    2. Center   4. Socialist   6. Christian   8. None of these
                                                      9. Don't know

118. Below are some income categories. In which of these categories would you estimate that your family's income of last year would fall?

                        1. Under 10,000
        2. Kr. 10,000 - 14,999   5. Kr. 25,000 - 29,999
        3. "   15,000 - 19,999   6. "   30,000 - 39,999
        4. "   20,000 - 24,999   7. "   40,000 - and over

119. What is the title of your father's present occupation? (Please be very specific)

120. How would you describe the work your father did during the greater part of your life? (Please circle only one)

    1. Worker (for example, in a factory, in lumbering, farm worker, seaman, fisherman, construction worker, etc.)
    2. White-collar worker (for example, as functionary or manager in office, commerce, industry, government bureau, etc.)
    3. Self-employed usually without other help (for example, a small farmer, fisherman, craftsman, small businessman, doctor, lawyer, etc.)
    4. Proprietor - self-employed usually with hired help (for example, farmer, businessman, industrialist, lawyer, etc.)

121. How do you expect your future standard of living (economic income) to compare with that of the family in which you were brought up?

    1. Higher standard
    2. About the same
    3. Lower standard

Please check and see if you have answered all questions

Date completed

HOLDNINGER BLANT STUDENTER

Spørsmålene i dette skjemaet er blitt besvart av studenter ved forskjellige universiteter i USA. Studentene har fortalt oss hvordan de ser på den verden de lever i, hvilke ting de ønsker å få ut av den, og hvorfor de ønsker dette. De har fortalt oss hva de mener om enkelte av sine institusjoner og om sine oppfatninger om utdannelse, karriere, arbeid, styreform, religion, og om krig og fred.

Dr. Jonassen, en sosiolog fra Ohio State University, er kommet til Norge med Fulbright-stipendium for å drive forskning. Han vil gjerne finne ut hvilke forskjeller og likheter som eksisterer mellom norske og amerikanske studenter med hensyn til deres meninger om disse emnene.

Både i USA og i Norge finner vi en høy grad av arbeidsdeling, og derfor har begge samfunn problemer med å rekruttere de rette personer til de mange forskjellige stillinger som eksisterer. Blant alle de muligheter som finnes kan det fra den enkeltes synspunkt ofte være vanskelig å velge nettopp det yrket som passer best for ham og hvor han kan bidra mest til det samfunn han lever i, foruten å utvikle sin egen personlighet. Ved å besvare disse spørsmålene kan De også hjelpe samfunnsforskere til å utvide sine kunnskaper som igjen kan komme yrkesveiledere til gode foruten at den enkelte blir bedre i stand til å velge det yrket han er best skikket til. Det er mulig at denne undersøkelsen kommer til å bli utvidet til også å omfatte andre land, slik at de generelle konklusjoner som eventuelt måtte bli resultatet av denne typen forskning, får større verdi fordi de er basert på data fra forskjellige kulturer.

Svarene på enkelte av disse spørsmålene kan kanskje virke opplagte for en nordmann, og enkelte andre spørsmål har muligens liten mening for en norsk student i det hele tatt. Men hvis vi skal kunne få et riktig grunnlag for sammenlikninger, må vi stille spørsmålene på samme måte som de ble stilt til amerikanske studenter. Vi håper derfor at De vil vise overbærenhet og svare på spørsmålene så godt som mulig.

Det finnes ingen riktige svar og studenter har alle slags oppfatninger om isse tingene. Vær så snill ikke å konferere med andre, det vi er interessert

er <u>Deres personlige oppfatning</u> om de emner som er behandlet i disse spørs-

nålene.

Besvarelsene skal være <u>anonyme</u> og kommer ikke til å bli satt i forbindel-

e med Dem eller Deres navn. Svarene vil bli behandlet utelukkende som

eler av en statistisk beskrivelse av grupper, og ingen enkelt persons menin-

er eller svar vil bli kjent.

Institutt for Samfunnsforskning, Oslo

The Ohio State University, Columbus, U.S.A.

Oslo 1962

NOEN GENERELLE RETNINGSLINJER FOR RESPONDENTENE

I dette spørreskjemaet er spørsmålene understreket med flere mulige nummererte svaralternativer under hvert spørsmål.

Vær så snill å lese hvert spørsmål grundig gjennom.

Les gjennom alle de svarmuligheter som står under hvert spørsmål.

Til hvert spørsmål eller spørsmålsgruppe er det en veiledning som ente står i parentes eller er understreket. Les dem grundig og følg dem nøye.

Avmerk så svaret på spørsmålet slik det er angitt i veiledningen, enten ved å sette en ring rundt nummeret på det svaret som passer best for Dem, eller som svarer best til Deres oppfatning, eller ved å gi den opplysning det spørres etter.

Hvis De skriver galt eller ønsker å skrive noe annet, kryss ut det gale svaret og skriv så det riktige.

Det er meget viktig for resultatene av denne undersøkelsen at De besvar er alle spørsmål så oppriktig som mulig.

Når De er ferdig med spørreskjemaet, vennligst les det gjennom for å se at De ikke har unnlatt å svare på noe.

En av våre medarbeidere vil oppsøke Dem i løpet av et par dager for å samle inn det utfylte spørreskjemaet.

Mange takk for hjelpen.

. Hvis De hadde fritt valg, hva ville
)e foretrekke å arbeide med når De
•r ferdig med Deres utdannelse?

Sett en ring bare rundt det De ville
ike best.)

. Egen forretning eller egen gård
. Egen privatpraksis (jurist, lege,
  tannlege ell. likn.)
. Undervisning
. Sosialt arbeid
. Annet organisasjonsarbeid
i. Offentlige kontor eller virksomhet
. Yrkesmilitær virksomhet
. Familieforetagende
•. Privat firma, aksjeselskap eller
  fabrikk
). Annet: (spesifiser:)

5-10 Hvilke tre ting i Deres fremtidige liv venter De størst tilfredsstil-
lelse av?

(Skriv 1 til venstre for det viktigste,
2 foran det nest viktigste og 3 foran
det tredje viktigste.)

Karriere eller yrke

Familieliv

Fritids- og feriebeskjeftigelser

Religiøs virksomhet

Deltakelse i samfunnslivet

Deltakelse i virksomhet som tar
sikte på å forbedre nasjonale eller
internasjonale forhold

1-22. Studenter har ulike meninger om de viktigste formål med universitets-
tdannelse. Noen av disse meningene er satt opp nedenfor. Når De leser
.enne listen, prøv da å tenke Dem hvilke formål det ideelle universitetet
•urde legge vekt på i sin undervisning. Avmerk Deres mening med å skrive:

  H (høy) foran de formål De mener er mest vesentlige for et universitet
  M (middels) foran de formål De mener er middels vesentlige
  L (lav) foran de formål De mener er uvesentlige, irrelevante eller til
  og med usmakelige. (Skriv H, M, L)

  A. "Sørge for yrkesutdannelse, utvikle kunnskaper og ferdigheter som
     kan anvendes direkte i Deres fremtidige yrke."

  B. "Utvikle Deres evne til å komme godt overens med forskjellige typer
     av mennesker."

  C. "Sørge for en grunnleggende almenutdannelse og gi et innblikk i ge-
     nerelle ideer."

  D. "Utvikle Deres kjennskap til og interesse for samfunns- og verdens-
     problemer."

  E. "Hjelpe Dem til å høyne Deres moralske nivå, Deres etiske standard
     og verdier."

  F. "Forberede Dem til et lykkelig ekteskap og familieliv."

iå så tilbake og ranger de formålene De har merket med H, ved å skrive:

  1 for det aller viktigste
  2 for det nest viktigste, osv.

3-42. Når studenter har gitt opplysninger om hvilke krav de stiller til det
deelle yrke eller stilling, har de sagt at det måtte tilfredsstille visse krav.
Ioen av disse kravene er stilt opp nedenfor. Når De leser denne listen,
•røv da å forestille Dem i hvilken grad et fag eller en yrkeskarriere må til-
redsstille hvert av disse kravene hvis De skulle anse det for ideelt.

Avmerk Deres mening ved å skrive:

H (høy) foran de krav De mener er mest vesentlige
M (middels) foran de krav De mener er middels vesentlige
L (lav) foran de krav De mener er uvesentlige, irrelevante eller til og
med usmakelige (skriv H, M, L.)

Den ideelle stilling for meg må ..... (Skriv H, M, L)

A. "Gi meg anledning til å bruke mine spesielle kunnskaper eller an-
legg. "

B. "Gi meg mulighet til å tjene mange penger. "

C. "Gi meg anledning til å være skapende og orginal. "

D. "Gi meg sosial prestisje. "

E. "Gi meg anledning til å arbeide med mennesker istedenfor ting. "

F. "Sette meg istand til å se frem til en stabil og sikker fremtid. "

G. "Gjøre meg relativt fri for overoppsyn fra andre. "

H. "Gi meg anledning til å lede andre. "

I. "Gi meg sjanse til å oppleve noe utenom det vanlige. "

J. "Gi meg anledning til å hjelpe andre. "

Gå så tilbake og ranger de kravene De har merket med H, ved å skrive

1 for det aller viktigste
2 for det nest viktigste, osv.

ved siden av hver H på listen. De skal ikke rangere de som er merket M og
L.

43-44. Hvilke to egenskaper på denne
listen kan etter Deres mening hjelpe
et ungt menneske til å komme seg hur-
tigst frem?

(Avmerk bare to.)

1. Hardt arbeid
2. Tiltalende vesen
3. Intelligens
4. Hensynsfullhet
5. Hell
6. Å være en god "politiker".

45. Hvis De kunne velge, hva av det
følgende ville De helst være?

(Avmerk bare en ting.)

1. Uavhengig, selvstendig

2. Fremgangsrik, (successful)

3. Godt likt

Er De enig eller uenig i de følgende uttalelser?

(Sett ring rundt "E" hvis De er enig, "U" hvis De er uenig og "?" hvis De ikke er sikker eller ikke har noen mening.)

46. Norge har det beste system for universitetsutdannelse ..... E ? U

47. Universitetsutdannelse bør være gratis for alle som har evner .... E ? U

48. Den beste regjering er den som regjerer minst .... E ? U

49. Fagforeningene her i landet gjør et utmerket arbeid .... E ? U

50. Regjeringsplanlegging fører nesten uomgjengelig til tap av den enkeltes rettigheter og frihet .... E ? U

51. Sosial rettferdighet kan bare oppnås i et sosialistisk land .... E ? U

52. Hvis folk er garantert en minimumslønn, kan de komme til å miste sin tiltakslyst .... E ? U

53. Den enkelte arbeidsgiver bør gi avkall på sin rett til å ansette og avsette uten hensyn til sosial velferd .... E ? U

54. Velferdsstaten har en tendens til å ødelegge den enkeltes initiativ.. E ? U

55. Det viktigste barn bør lære er lydighet og respekt for sine foresatte .... E ? U

56. Demokratiets grunnlag er avhengig av at samfunnet gir muligheter for fritt initiativ i forretningslivet............. E ? U

57. En universitetsutdannelse bidrar mer til å bryte ned verdier enn til å bygge opp idealer..................... E ? U

58. Statens lover for fagforeningens virksomhet er ikke strenge nok .... E ? U

59. Trass i alle våre anstrengelser for å fremme fred, kan nasjoner rett og slett ikke leve fredelig sammen, så vi kan like godt regne med en krig med få års mellomrom ... E ? U

60. Hvis det ikke er satt noen øvre grenser for forretningsprofitt, er det bedre muligheter til å produsere varer til lavere pris.. E ? U

61. Menneskeliv er altfor dyrebare til å ofres for å opprettholde noen regjeringsform .... E ? U

62. En nasjons rettigheter er bestemt av den makt nasjonen har E ? U

63. Et samfunn bør <u>garantere</u> at enhver får en akseptabel levestandard. . . . . E ? U

64. Personer som agiterer for fred er stort sett uansvarlige idealister. . . . . E ? U

65. Både krig og fred er nødvendige for fremskrittet . . . . E ? U

66. Politisk valgte representanter er som regel i hendene på spesielle interesser . . . . E ? U

67. Jeg anser kirken for å være en skadelig institusjon som fremmer sneversyn, fanatisme og intoleranse . . . . . . E ? U

68. Jeg ser kirken som et svært viktig middel til å høyne menneskenes liv i verden i dag . . . . E ? U

69. Jeg føler behov for å tro på en eller annen form for religiøs retning eller filosofi . . . . E ? U

70. Mitt religiøse samfunn har noe eget ved seg, noe som står over og høyere enn det enkelte medlem . . . . E ? U

71. Det er liten nytte i å henvende seg til offentlige personer, fordi de ofte ikke har virkelig interesse for den jevne manns problemer . . . . E ? U

72. Vanlige mennesker er ikke kvalifiserte til å stemme over våre dagers kompliserte spørsmål . . . . E ? U

73. Politiske kandidater er som regel dirigert av det politiske apparat . . . . E ? U

74. Jeg tror universitetslærere er redd for å si hva de virkelig mener nå for tiden . . . . E ? U

75. Det meste av det jeg lærer på universitetet, er umaken verd . . . . E ? U

76. Jeg mener at jeg nå har et tilstrekkelig religiøst eller filosofisk grunnlag som rettesnor for min oppførsel . . . . . E ? U

77. Det virker som om alt i våre dager er mer eller mindre korrupt (a racket). . . . . E ? U

78. Jeg føler meg ofte ensom sammen med andre mennesker . . . . E ? U

79. Siden livet er så kort, kan vi like godt spise, drikke og være glade . . . . E ? U

80. Jeg oppdager at jeg for tiden ofte mister troen på at jeg skal bli til noe . . . . E ? U

31. Når det kommer til stykket, er det ingen som kommer
til å bry seg om hva som skjer med deg .... E ? U

32. Hvis du ikke passer deg, vil folk komme til å utnytte
deg... E ? U

33. Menneskets natur er i bunn og grunn innstilt på sam-
arbeid .... E ? U

34. Jeg har som regel ikke nok tillit til meg selv........... E ? U

35. Jeg blir ubehagelig berørt hvis noen kritiserer meg, uan-
sett hvem det er .... E ? U

36. Hvis en skal komme seg frem i våre dager, nytter det
ikke å være prippen med de midler en bruker .... E ? U

Sett en ring rundt tallet foran det utsagnet som best gir uttrykk for Deres
mening eller som passer best for Dem.)

37. Noen sier at de fleste mennesker er til å stole på, andre sier at en
kan ikke være for forsiktig i sitt samvær med andre mennesker. Hva
mener De om dette?

    1.   De fleste mennesker er til å stole på

    2.   En kan ikke være for forsiktig

38. Vil De si at de fleste mennesker er mest innstilt på å hjelpe andre
eller mest innstilt på å sørge for seg selv?

    1.   Hjelpe andre

    2.   Sørge for seg selv

39. Hvordan vil De si at De føler Dem vanligvis - i godt humør eller i
dårlig humør?

    1.   Meget godt humør   4.   Nokså dårlig humør
    2.   Nokså godt humør   5.   Meget dårlig humør
    3.   Hverken godt eller dårlig

40. Er De et slikt menneske som bekymrer Dem eller bekymrer De Dem
ikke?

    1.   Bekymrer meg svært mye   3.   Bekymrer meg litt
    2.   Bekymrer meg nokså mye   4.   Bekymrer meg ikke

41. Hvor viktig er det for Dem personlig å komme frem i livet?

    1.   Meget viktig   3.   Ikke særlig viktig
    2.   Nokså viktig   4.   Ikke viktig i det hele tatt

92. <u>Føler De noen gang at politiske eller offentlige forhold angår Dem like</u> <u>mye som forhold i Deres eget liv?</u>

    1. Ja
    2. Nei

93. <u>Vil De si at De har lettere eller vanskeligere for å vinne venner enn</u> <u>de fleste mennesker?</u>

    1. Lettere
    2. Omtrent det samme
    3. Vanskeligere

94. <u>Hvor viktig er det for Dem å være godt likt av forskjellige typer men-</u> <u>nesker?</u>

    1. Svært viktig   3. Ikke særlig viktig
    2. Nokså viktig   4. Svært uviktig

95. <u>Er det ubehagelig for Dem at et annet menneske gir Dem ordrer?</u>

    1. Meget ubehagelig
    2. Litt ubehagelig
    3. Ikke ubehagelig

96. <u>Er det ubehagelig for Dem å gi ordrer til et annet menneske?</u>

    1. Meget ubehagelig
    2. Litt ubehagelig
    3. Ikke ubehagelig

97. <u>Foretrekker De å treffe avgjørelser selv eller foretrekker De å la</u> <u>andre treffe avgjørelser når De er i en gruppe?</u>

    1. Foretrekker som regel å treffe avgjørelser selv
    2. Foretrekker som regel å la andre treffe avgjørelser
    3. Er ikke sikker på hva jeg foretrekker

98. <u>Hvor viktig er det for Dem å ha klare fremtidsplaner?</u>

    1. Meget viktig
    2. Stort sett viktig, relativt viktig
    3. Ikke særlig viktig, helt uviktig

99. <u>Hva synes De er den beste måten en nasjon kan utføre sine rakett- og</u> <u>romeksperimenter på?</u>

    1. Utføre eksperimenter i hemmelighet så langt det er mulig og bare offentliggjøre dem hvis og når de er vellykket

    2. Utføre alle eksperimenter åpent med full publisitet, slik at både de mislykte og de vellykte blir kjent

3. Den ene måten er like god som den andre

101. Hvilken av disse to tror De personlig er den mest effektive krigshemmende faktor?

    1. Atombomben
    2. De Forente Nasjoner

102. Mener De det ville være verdt å føre en total krig for å stanse kommunismen, eller mener De at en total krig for å stanse kommunismen ikke ville være verdt å føre?

    1. Absolutt verdt å føre   4. Absolutt ikke verdt å føre
    2. Stort sett neppe verdt å føre 5. Intet svar, usikker
    3. Neppe verdt å føre

103. Hvilket av de følgende utsagn beskriver best Deres følelse om det guddommelige?

    1. Jeg tror på Gud, universets skaper, som kjenner mine innerste tanker og følelser, og som jeg en dag skal stå til rette for.

    2. Jeg tror på en makt som er høyere enn meg selv, som noen mennesker kaller Gud og som noen mennesker kaller Naturen.

    3. Jeg tror på menneskeverdet, men ikke på Gud eller på et høyere Vesen.

    4. Jeg tror på naturretten og at det som kalles tilværelsens mysterier en gang kan klarlegges ved hjelp av vitenskapelige metoder.

    5. Jeg er ikke sikker på hva jeg tror på.

    6. Jeg er ateist.

(Sett ring rundt det svaret som passer for Dem, eller skriv de opplysningene det spørres om på den plassen som er satt av.)

104. I hvilket fakultet er De innskrevet?

    1. Det teologiske   3. Det medisinske   5. Det realvitenskapelige
    2. Det juridiske   4. Det historisk-filosofiske   6. Det odontologiske

104. Hva er Deres hovedfag eller spesialfag? _____

105. Hvilken stilling tar De sikte på? _____

106. Hvilket universitetsår er dette for Dem?

    Første, annet, tredje, fjerde, femte, mer

107. Hvor mange år har De studert eller lært engelsk? _____

108. Alder sist fødselsdag _____

109. Kjønn: 1. Mann   2. Kvinne

110. Ekteskapelig status: 1. Ugift   3. Skilt
                             2. Gift   4. Enke/enkemann

111. Hvor er De vokst opp?

    1. I storby (5 største)   4. På landet
    2. I småby   5. Vekslende mellom forskjel-
    3. I tettbygd strøk på   lige av disse steder
       landet

112. Navnet på hjemstedsfylke _____

113. Hvor har De bodd den største del av Deres liv?

    1. Østlandet   3. Sørlandet   5. Nord-Norge
    2. Vestlandet   4. Trøndelag   6. Utlandet

114. Hvilken religion har De?   _____

115. I hvilken av disse tre sosiale gruppene mener De Deres familie hører
     til?

    1. Høyere sosial status (Upper class)
    2. Middels sosial status (Middle class)
    3. Lavere sosial status (Working class)

116. Hvilket politisk parti mener De representerer Deres politiske syn best?

    1. DNA   3. NKP   5. Høyre   7. Venstre   9. Vet ikke
    2. Senter   4. SF   6. Kr.F.   8. Ingen av
                                         dem

117. Hvilket politisk parti mener De representerer Deres fars politiske syn
     best?

    1. DNA   3. NKP   5. Høyre   7. Venstre   9. Vet ikke
    2. Senter   4. SF   6. Kr.F.   8. Ingen av
                                         dem

118. I hvilken av disse inntektsgruppene ville De anslå Deres fars inntekt
     siste år til å være?

                    1. Under 10.000

    2. Kr. 10.000 - 14.999   5. Kr. 25.000 - 29.999
    3.   "   15.000 - 19.999   6.   "   30.000 - 39.999
    4.   "   20.000 - 24.999   7.   "   40.000 - og over

19. Hva er tittelen på Deres fars nåværende stilling?   (Vær så snill å gi en meget presis angivelse.)

20. Hvordan vil De beskrive det arbeidet Deres far hadde størsteparten av Deres liv?   (Sett ring bare rundt en kategori.)

    1. Arbeider (f. eks. i en fabrikk, i skogen, i jordbruket, sjømann, fisker uten egen båt, bygningsarbeider etc.)

    2. Funksjonær (f. eks. funksjonær eller formann på et kontor, i handel, industri, offentlig virksomhet etc.)

    3. Selvstendig uten leiet hjelp (f. eks. småbruker, fisker, håndverker, kjøpmann, lege, sakfører, etc.)

    4. Selvstendig med leiet hjelp (f. eks. bonde, forretningsmann, fabrikkeier, advokat etc.)

21. Hvordan regner De med at Deres fremtidige levestandard (økonomisk sett) kommer til å bli i forhold til levestandarden i den familie hvor De vokste opp?

    1. Min levestandard blir høyere
    2. Min levestandard blir omtrent den samme
    3. Min levestandard blir lavere

Vær så snill å lese igjennom spørreskjemaet og se om De har besvart alle spørsmålene.

Utfylt den